Getting Started in Home Education

Mary Ann Rose

and

Paul Stanbrook

Published 2000 by Education Now Publishing Co-operative Ltd.
113 Arundel Drive, Bramcote Hills, Nottingham NG9 3FQ
in partnership with Herald

British Cataloguing in Publication Data

Rose, Mary Ann and Stanbrook, Paul
        Getting Started in Home Education

ISBN 1-871526-42-6

Further cataloguing details are available from the British Library

Rear cover photograph: Rebecca Northway,
                Lookinglass Photographic Studio, Cheltenham

Design and production: Paul Stanbrook with Education Now

Printed by Mastaprint Ltd., Sandiacre, Nottingham, NG10 5HU

The Schoolboy

I love to rise on a summer morn,
When the birds sing on every tree;
The distant huntsman winds his horn,
And the skylark sings with me;
Oh, what sweet company!

But to go to school on a summer morn, -
Oh it drives all joy away!
Under a cruel eye outworn
The little ones spend the day
In sighing and dismay.

Ah then at times I drooping sit,
And spend many an anxious hour;
Nor in my book can I take delight,
Nor sit in learning's bower,
Worn through with the dreary shower.

How can the bird that is born for joy
Sit in a cage and sing?
How can a child, when fears annoy,
But droop his tender wing,
And forget his youthful spring?

Oh father and mother, if buds are nipped,
And blossoms blown away;
And if the tender plants are stripped
Of their joy in the springing day,
By sorrow and care's dismay, -

How shall the summer arise in joy,
Or the summer fruits appear?
Or how shall we gather what griefs destroy,
Or bless the mellowing year,
When the blasts of winter appear?

William Blake, Songs of Experience 1794

The Authors

Paul Stanbrook and Mary Ann Rose have home-educated their children in West Gloucestershire for many years. Mary Ann worked as a class teacher and Special Needs teacher in state schools for fifteen years before leaving to bring up their family. Paul is a consultant in the computer industry. He has a personal interest in music and classical languages.

Preface

This book was written to help both established and new home educators, and to give advice and guidance to those who may be considering de-registering a child from the school system.

The information and suggested methods of organisation and teaching may also be of interest to professional teachers and educationalists, and those who are considering a career in teaching or working with groups of children.

This book is based on the legal and educational situation in England, Wales and Scotland at the time of writing. Readers in other parts of the world will undoubtedly find much of worth in the book but allowances should be made for statutory and cultural differences.

For ease of reading, the term parent should be taken to include legal guardian, and the masculine gender he/him/his has been used to cover either sex. Similarly, the singular child has been used, but should be taken to mean the plural where relevant.

While all reasonable care has been given to ensure the accuracy of the information in this book we cannot accept legal responsibility for any errors or omissions within it.

Acknowledgements

We should like to acknowledge the help and support of our own children, Joe, Ned, Ben, Polly and Kester in the production of this book.

Special thanks go to Roland and Janet Meighan for their inspiration, and to Ian Dowty for his part in looking over the legal aspects. We also appreciate the part played by Alex Lester whose early morning radio programme has helped us to retain our sanity and sense of humour.

We also wish to thank the many supportive people who, having got to know our children, will testify to the success of home education.

Contents

List Of Figures

Home educators start with the child

Chapter One

Introduction To Home Education

ή γαρ ού χρη ποιεισθαι παιδας ή συνδιαταλαιπωρειν και τρεθοντα και παιδευοντα.

Plato - Crito

Either we should not bring children into the world or we ought to persevere to the end in bringing them up and educating them.

Tr. P.S.

Home Education

It is legal; you are not alone; your child will not lose out; and you can do it, even if you are not a teacher. Opting for home education is, however, an enormous decision that will affect your home life for many years and it will change your child's life. Forever.

Over the years that we have been actively involved, we have talked to home-educating families across the whole spectrum of society - rich and poor, young and old, city and country. Some had already decided never to send their as yet unborn children to school, others have removed fifteen-year-olds from school due to unbearable problems within the school system, with less than a year to go before their GCSE examinations. The phenomenon seems to be international, judging from the enquiries we have had from all parts of the globe. In fact, the only thing that home-educating families have in common is that they are each unique.

Baobab tree, drawn by a home-educated child living in Kenya

The decision to home-educate may not be irrevocable. Some parents, on trying home education, find that for one reason or another it is not working. In these cases, children return to school, hopefully with any problem resolved. On the other hand, for one reason or another it may not be possible or desirable for the child to return to school.

Our aim in this book is not to persuade you that you should remove your child from school. For many families, school is the best option and we should be very wrong to decry that. The object of this book is to give you the information that will help you to make an informed decision, to help you to get along with Local Education Authorities (LEAs) and to guide you in practical aspects of getting started in home education.

This Book

This book was written in response to a need by both incipient home educators and parents considering alternatives to state education. After this introductory chapter we explore the possibility of resolving problems which may have arisen at school and we look at the alternatives to the state school system, of which home education is only one. Chapter 3 deals with the many aspects of home education, both for and against which may influence your decision. If you have already made your decision, however, then you may wish to skip directly to the fourth chapter where you are guided through the minefield of developing a philosophy which may well involve turning your latent and subconscious ideals into a palpable statement. Chapter 5 looks at the legal aspects of home education and discusses relationships with Local Education Authorities.

Chapter 6 shows how you would begin what may be a very daunting task - taking on the role of teacher, but maybe reassessing your view of what a teacher is. In the next chapter a suggested scheme of education is presented. Of course you are under no obligation to follow this scheme, but many have already found it a useful way of applying a structure to the situation without imposing a straitjacket. In the next chapter we look at specific subject areas and particular aspects which apply to them. The book ends with a list of useful contacts and resources.

Definition

The legal requirement is education. The child does not have to attend school; neither does education necessarily have to take place in the home; however, when parents remove children from the school system - state or otherwise - the responsibility for the children's education lies with them.

The education that we give our own children is based in the home; the children's books, writing materials and reference literature are mostly at home, and most of their writing is done at home. It is very much inspired and dependant upon experiences in the real world, however - we use libraries, environmental education sites, shopping trips, indeed every opportunity possible to extend and develop the education of the children. In reality home is only a base from which to learn.

For many, the term *school* conjures up early memories of sitting in rows, behind desks, with the teacher at the front expounding his specialised subject under the heading of History, Maths or Music. When forty-five minutes of History is over, it is time to troop to another classroom for a similar session of, say, English. As home-educators, however, we prefer to educate our children in a much wider sense, partly by integrating subjects of study, and partly by including such activities as cooking, housework and gardening as part of the overall curriculum.

The natural reaction on being given a new idea is to attach it to a familiar concept. This is why the popular image of a robot is anthropoid - shaped and behaving distinctively like a human, albeit with a few significant differences, although in practice robots can be any size, shape or form, but very rarely having faces. In the same way, a common perception of home education is one of a classroom in a house where lessons and exercise books prevail until 3:15 each weekday. The reality is often very different, as this book will show. For us, home *education* is what it is all about; home *schooling* is not a term we particularly care to use.

School is the institution;

education is the objective.

Background To Home Education

The precedent for home education lies in the thousands of years of human civilisation and its achievements, not in the increasingly narrow viewpoint and detailed legislation which governments have imposed in the short period since the advent of state schools.

From antiquity Jewish children were taught by their fathers. The entire literature of the Old Testament was produced before Jewish elementary schools were established. The word *school* only appears once in the whole Bible. Acts 19:9 refers to a Graeco-Roman school which grew up following Hellenistic infiltration into Jewish Society.

Throughout history, many significant people were, like William Blake, Charles Dickens and Siegfried Sassoon, home-educated. In our own times, Gerald Durrell and Yehudi Menuhin are just two personalities who were not educated at school.

Only a few decades ago it was normal for families of the aristocracy to employ a Governess who was responsible for the elementary education of the children until they were sent away to a boarding school. This approach is still available to those who can afford it. For many years the children of the Australian outback have been taught using radio links with a teacher many miles away. Advertisements for correspondence courses have appeared in our newspapers for as long as we can remember. There is nothing new about the idea of learning outside a school's walls.

Nowadays information and access to specialists across the world are available in our own homes through television, radio and the Internet. Information and communication are key words in today's technological world.

Many parents who are joining the band of home educators now are taking the revolution in IT to heart. We were asked recently, *"Why can't my daughter work entirely from home, speaking to, let's say, a professor at Harvard on the Internet if she is doing a project on astronomy?"* The answer is there is no reason at all, providing the professor has the time and inclination to contact every child who calls him on the Internet. Schools link up to each other and compare studies from region to region already, using modems and faxes. When the Internet is available in every school, no doubt this practice will become even more commonplace.

> *And these words, which I command thee this day, shall be in thine heart: and thou shalt teach them diligently unto thy children, and shalt talk of them when thou sittest in thine house, and when thou walkest by the way, and when thou liest down, and when thou risest up.*
> **Deuteronomy 6:6-7 AV**

The Queen didn't go to School

Internet technology should be a facility which home educators use to their advantage. Already many home-educating families use it regularly, and the *virtual school* where information is shared and exchanged through home computers has become reality.

Distance learning is more popular than ever. It is possible to take a degree course without leaving your own home through the Open University. Now there is also the Open College, as well as numerous distance courses for GCSE subjects and specialist studies. Schools no longer have the monopoly on education. Indeed, the quality of education outside schools may be superior to their own.

Since taking our own children out of school and embarking on home education some five years ago, we have been contacted by many parents. They are either considering home education or they about to do the same, and are in desperate need of practical help. Putting a stop to school may solve some problems, but how can that form of education be replaced? How do parents set about becoming teachers? What materials and resources are available to families? Where does specialist help come from if needed? Are there any other home educators in the area, and how can they be contacted? How can one Mum be a full-time teacher, get the housework done and dinner on the table? (Although many home-educating fathers are actively involved, frequently it is the mother who has the primary role of educator.)

When writing a book which sets out to justify a system which flies in the face of accepted practice there is always a danger that the writers will be interpreted as severe critics of the orthodox system, in this case, schools. Our own experiences of our separate schools were generally quite satisfactory, even though we might now question "what might have been".

In Mary Ann's case, had she been desperately miserable it is unlikely that she would have later decided to train as a teacher and to voluntarily return to those institutions. Schools provided her with a living for many years, and it was through working in schools, observing and listening to experienced teachers that she learnt her craft. It was also through intimate contact with schools and all who dwell in them that the seeds of doubt were sown.

For of all sad words of tongue or pen,

The saddest are these: "It might have been!"
John Greenleaf Whittier

In justifying and presenting the evidence for home education we draw comparisons between schools as we have experienced them (as pupil, parent and teacher) and our experience of home education as home-educating parents, through working with and for home-educating families, and through research. There are flaws in the school system, and schools do behave in strange ways sometimes, leaving parents and pupils mystified as to the true nature of the education which is being offered. As far as possible we have tried to put the case from both sides of the desk. To be fair, the logistics of keeping a group of at least a hundred - maybe a thousand or more - children safe, in one place and instilling a form of education which has been imposed by central government for five hours a day, five days a week may account for the behaviour of the schools and the teachers. This is not to say that schools and all in them are bad - far from it. What is stressed throughout this book is that there is more than one way to educate and to learn.

Home educators have much to learn from experienced teachers and much to learn from schools. Hopefully, as awareness of the merits and possibility of home education is raised, schools will realise that they may have something to learn from home educators.

School life suits many children; it also suits many parents that their children attend school. There is no shame in this. The emphasis in this book is upon individuality and choice. Success in home education depends upon a) enjoyment of being and learning with your own children and b) the acknowledgement and respect for the individuality of each child. This is the basis upon which home educators build. We put the child first, watch, listen and learn from him, and build upon that which the child teaches us about himself.

> *What we want to see is the child in pursuit of knowledge, not knowledge in pursuit of the child.*
> **George Bernard Shaw**

Schools, on the other hand, start with a prescription from the government and a mass of raw materials - children. Their task is to match the two and to get a result at the end of the year/Key Stage/educational career.

Two very different systems, described from personal experience of both. Without knowledge or recent experience of either system it is easy to be dazzled and confused. In today's competitive world schools present us with glossy brochures, guided tours, attractive displays and banks of computer technology. We are shown facilities and equipment unavailable to an ordinary household. Like a great hypermarket, a school seems to offer everything from swimming pools to microscopes, from tubas to plasticine, all in one convenient package - the school campus. Home by comparison takes on the appearance of a corner shop - open all hours! Yet home educators tell of children who pass A-levels at the age of five or six, who are accepted for universities at ten, who carry off prizes in national music competitions.

The message of this book is that the choice is yours. The purpose of the book is to empower the reader with knowledge to make an educated choice. The information and exercises in this book will help you to develop your own ideas about education, what it means to you and whether your family are suited to a home-based education.

Our Own Story

Mary Ann had trained as a teacher, and worked for about fifteen years when our eldest son was rising five. We had some doubts about the ways in which schools operated, and did not agree with all of the changes which were taking place in State education, but we decided to give school a try, and Joe was looking forward to going. He had been into schools before, and to the child a classroom looked an exciting place, and somewhere he could have some company. Joe was able to read before he started school. He had always loved stories and books, and reading had come very naturally to him. We told the school that Joe was reading when we went to register him and we showed the teachers his reading books.

After two weeks at school, the child was still being given picture books and had not been asked to read at anything approaching the level of which he was capable. We spoke to the class teacher about this, but made little progress. Meanwhile, Joe was becoming more uncomfortable about school. He found the other children aggressive, and the tasks he was expected to do easy. It was not long before it became clear to us all that school was not living up to our expectations, nor was it providing an education appropriate to the 'age and ability' of our son. Still, we felt he was getting to mix with other children, and learning some social skills, so he stayed in school.

After Christmas, things changed. Joe became increasingly unhappy about school. He took on the appearance of a pubescent teenager, slouching into school instead of skipping (children skip when they are happy), and it became increasingly difficult to get him up and ready for school each morning. His behaviour towards his younger brothers became more aggressive, causing the younger children to be distressed and bewildered, and aggressive in return. Then Joe started to have nightmares, and began sleepwalking. He also complained of tummy aches, often first thing in the morning and on school days.

The GP was consulted, and found nothing physical wrong with the child. She suggested that the symptoms might be caused by stress. The work which Joe was given at school had kept pace with the rest of his year group, but was still hardly approaching the level he had been at in September. We made an appointment with the school again, and saw both the Head teacher and the class teacher, but it became clear that the situation in school would not be changing very fast, if at all.

At the half-term break in February, Joe celebrated his fifth birthday, and at Easter he left school to be educated at home. We took the decision reluctantly, as we had had high hopes that Joe would do well in school. He was a bright and keen little boy, and enthusiastic, so it was heartbreaking to see how quickly all that disappeared once he went to school. We hoped that the difficulties he had experienced would be transitory, and that perhaps he would enjoy school again in a year or two.

So when Joe's younger brother, Ned, started school two years later, both boys went together. Ned also looked forward to going to school, but when he experienced problems he rebelled in a different way. Ned simply refused to go. As he opened his eyes in the morning he would say, "I don't want to go to school today, thank you". From that moment, we knew we had a fight on our hands! Ned was a big lad for four years old, and it was not easy to carry him into school, kicking and screaming. We would telephone the school, who sent two strong ladies out onto the playground to meet us and carry the child in, where they would contain him, grumbling, crying and kicking in rage, until he calmed down. Usually by mid morning he had become reasonable enough to join in with the class. When he came back home, he would then ask to do some work, and we would find some writing or sums, and hear him read a book from home. Next morning, we went through the whole pantomime again.

Of course, all this had an effect on Joe, and between the two of them we were lucky if we got through one day each week when they went to school without a scene. Poor Ben (aged 3) witnessed the scenes from his car seat every morning, and must have thought, "This is what school is like. Next year it will be me!"

We went back to the doctor, and had the same reply as before. We went back to the school several times. After Joe's SATS tests, we saw the class teacher and the Head, and heard that he had underachieved. We questioned some of the teaching and Joe's social skills, and were told that his problem is that *he reads too much*, and then, "Home life is too interesting. That's why he doesn't want to come to school."

At the time we were astonished. We did not make a fuss, we just wrote to the school and took both the boys out. They had lasted two terms.

Since then, we have taught the children at home. We have also learned that we are far from being the only ones who are told that their children read too much, or that their home is too interesting. This has happened to many people.

We do not believe that the school which our children attended was to blame for their failure within the system. The school and the staff did their very best to settle our children and showed only kindness and patience with our boys. It is the system and the demands imposed combined with the financial restraints placed upon schools which caused the overall problem. Had our children been given sufficient time and adequate resources, both human and material, our story might have continued in a different way. We are not alone in our dissatisfaction of the school system. What we did have, however, was the knowledge, courage and ability to make a choice.

> *... it was the setting, not the learning itself, that was the problem...*
> *"I wasn't turned off education at all - it was just the school." -* *Kate*
> **Julie Webb, Those Unschooled Minds**

Before taking the children out of school altogether we looked at a range of other schools, larger and smaller, private and State, and we came to the conclusion that essentially there was not a school that would be very different available to us. We saw some very good State schools which would have been excellent if allowed a little more freedom and imagination. We saw some private schools with interesting but unworkable philosophies for children in the 1990s. In the end we decided that anything school could do, we could do equally as well if not better.

Fifteen years ago teachers were still allowed some spontaneity. A child would arrive in the morning with a flower, and in taking the time to admire the gift and talk about its colour, shape, and all those interesting things inside the bloom, a more effective biology lesson was given than many which had been scrupulously planned and illustrated with numerous worksheets or chalkboard diagrams.

Much of this spontaneity has been extinguished over the last few years. Deadlines must now be met, little boxes in record books filled with satisfactory ticks - set tasks completed by certain dates. Should a child miss school through sickness, for example, the class will press on. No doubt subjects are repeated, but if the first lesson has been missed, it is sometimes very hard to catch up. There seems to be no time to stop, or go a little slower for those who did not get the idea the first time, no time to consider things which are not included in the Great Scheme, no time to 'stand and stare.' Yet so much can be gained from a bit of standing and staring.

It was the sense of wonder and delight, the chance to enjoy a childhood free from adult worries, the opportunity to learn in a natural and unhurried way, and to nurture relationships within a secure family and circle of friends which we wanted for our children. This is what home education has achieved for us. We are pleased when we hear comments praising our children's manners, the children seem to be quite bright, and they show respect and consideration for each other and their neighbours. For us, home education has definitely worked.

Chapter Two

When School Does Not Work

Obest plerumque iis qui discere volunt auctoritas eorum qui se docere profitentur.

Cicero, De Natura Deorum

The authority of those who profess to teach usually obstructs those who wish to learn.

Tr. P.S.

The School System

Schools and state education can be traced back to antiquity, although the Cretan gymnasia were not attended by youths until they were aged seventeen. Over 2500 years ago Spartan children were taken by the state into boarding schools with tough regimes unimaginable today. Greek schools, specialising in politics, philosophy and rhetoric and typified by those of Plato, Aristotle and Isocrates, were emulated by the Romans and thus spread throughout Western Europe. With the collapse of the Roman Empire in 476 AD, academic expertise remained only in the monasteries for six or seven hundred years, before the foundation of the first universities. Monasteries were considered a training ground rather than a refuge in Norman times. Throughout this period and, indeed, up to the nineteenth century, education was only available to the privileged few. The introduction of compulsory education has been a slow process, from the Factory Act of 1802 where children apprenticed in factories were to be taught the three R's, up to the Education Act of 1944 where the system of secondary education for all was established.

Most modern schools were introduced in this country over a century ago and have fundamentally changed little since that time. The quality of education received in schools has been questioned, and the school system may produce some undesirable effects in children. It is probably fair to say that at some time, every parent wonders if it is really in their child's best interests to keep him at the school he is in. Many home educators believe that the school system is now outdated and outmoded, and that they can do anything as well as schools, often better.

During their school career, most children experience some unhappy times at school, perhaps there is a clash of personalities between the child and the class teacher, or friendships amongst peer groups which wane and change. The work may be pitched at the wrong level for the child, causing distress and anxiety, or perhaps a lack of motivation results in poor academic performance. The school's approach to discipline may be a contentious issue - many new home educators complain of a lack of discipline in schools, which fails to stop bullying.

Some of these causes for anxiety on behalf of parents and children are transitory and will resolve themselves. It is part of life to encounter people whom we do not get on with, or authority with which we have to comply, like it or not.

At some point, however, the stress experienced by children in school may become too much for the family or the child to bear. It is at this stage that parents consider whether the child might be better off at home and if they could not do the job of teaching him as well as the school if not better themselves. Child stress should never be disparaged. At present in the UK there is reckoned to be one suicide of a school-age child every month.

Resolving The Problem

When it is apparent that things are going wrong in some way at school, parents have the right to know what is happening and why. There are set procedures, a sequence of events which can, and should, be followed if you have reason for complaint, or would like some explanation as to what is happening in school.

If you or your child experience difficulties at school these procedures are outlined in the following paragraphs, together with the writers' recommendations of the action which you might be advised to take throughout.

First, make an appointment to see the class teacher or tutor, preferably after school when they will have sufficient time to devote to your complaints. If possible, attend the meeting without the child, but with a partner or friend who will be able to support you and to discuss with you the issues raised later. Have a clear idea of the points which you want to raise at the meeting, and keep it objective. Personal comments are neither helpful or necessary, so try to remain pleasant and polite whilst putting your case firmly. You might like to take a notepad and record what is said during the meeting. Ask the teacher what they intend to do about your complaints, and agree when you expect to see some improvements to the situation. You might like to make another appointment for, perhaps, two weeks' time, when you can discuss the issue again.

It is only fair on the teacher to allow some time for whatever is wrong to be put right, and fair on your child to allow him time to work through a difficult situation, so try to aim for this. Stay calm, even if you feel furious, and do not feel intimidated when you go into school for this meeting; the teacher will probably feel every bit as nervous about this meeting as you do.

Take some time to write up a brief résumé of the meeting as soon as possible afterwards. Make a copy and keep it safe somewhere, and remember to put a date and time on it.

If you have not already done so, start keeping a diary in which you can make a note of any recurrence of the issues which caused the problem at school in the first place. This will be your evidence and may be helpful later if the problem is not resolved.

Having given the class teacher plenty of opportunity to remedy the situation, if things do not show any sign of improvement, your next step is to take the matter up with the Head of Department, or the Head Teacher, or both. Again, make an appointment to see them, rather than going in to the office and demanding an interview, or talking on the telephone. Take your partner or a friend so that you have a witness to the conversation, and be prepared with questions, notes, dates and times of your grievances. Once again, write up your notes from the meeting as a record. If you get no joy in the response this time, write to the school Governors.

The governing body of a school is ultimately responsible for the way in which the school is run, and the Head is answerable to the governors. In the first place, you might consider raising the issue with one of the parent governors, who should be able to advise you upon the best course of action. If you write to the governors your grievances can be discussed at a meeting, and a course of action decided upon. They should inform you of any decision taken at the meeting.

If, after all this, things from your end are no better, it may be time to consider removing the child from that school. You do not have to go through the entire process described above before removing a child from school. The whole thing could take a very long time, during which time your child must continue attending the school. A miserable day at school, however, is a very long time for a young child. Half a term is only about six weeks, not a long time in terms of giving it a chance and the next Governors' meeting, but a lifetime if you are a victim of bullying. All too frequently, it is only when a child threatens suicide or runs away that the true magnitude of the fear which they are experiencing is understood by parents and schools.

Maybe the stress school incurs is too great to bear, and you opt to take your child out of school before completing the whole course of set procedures. You have every right to do so. The main thing is that you feel that you have given schooling a chance, and are convinced that, even if you can do no better at education than the school, you can certainly do no worse.

Talk about the options open to you with your child, and listen to his opinion whilst making up your mind. Children have a knack of turning the most well-meaning decisions of their parents round and blaming adults for the way things turn out. The child's simpler view of the situation may make you realise that you have not seen the wood for the trees. Find out about alternative options, find out about what home education really means and explain these to your child. Listen to what the child wants and encourage him to express any fears he may have. This requires patience, time and space. Take his opinions into account when considering a plan of action and try to find a solution which will be mutually satisfactory. The last thing you need is to start by feeling guilty yourself.

Home education is legal, but no matter how bad things get at school, parents cannot simply keep children at home. This may invoke action being taken against them for breach of the truancy law. In order to home-educate, a child must be formally deregistered from school.

Flexi-Schooling

When traditional schooling does not work it may be worth considering the alternatives before opting for home education.

Is there, for example, any possibility of part-time attendance at school, or flexi-schooling? Flexi-schooling is legal and it is possible at the discretion of the Head Teacher of the school.

Any 'school age' child who goes to school at all must attend regularly, but absence 'with leave' does not count as irregular attendance. During such absences the child is officially at school, but is effectively being educated off site. (S)he is therefore covered for insurance and attracts full funding. Such arrangements are at the discretion of the school, (s444(9)).
S444 (3) (a) 1996 Education Act

Many will not entertain the idea, but there is some evidence that a gradual change is taking place. Human Scale Education have advocated the need for flexi-schooling for many years and may be able to advise on the current situation in your area. Sometimes flexi-schooling can be negotiated between parents and the Head, and in some areas the LEA home education manager will negotiate flexi-schooling with schools. This approach may benefit to some children who might otherwise be very isolated at home or very distressed in school full-time. It can give home-educating parents some relief from continual child care and support in the education of the child. More than this, it can be beneficial to participating schools, as the child will be registered so the school should receive the capitation allowance for the child.

Other Schools

The full magnitude of the decision to home-educate is discussed in greater detail in Chapter 3. It is a decision which will affect your whole family and every aspect of your lives, so before taking the enormous step of deregistration it is worth considering the educational provision offered by other schools. The following paragraphs suggest a number of questions which you might address when looking around. We offer no answers to these questions - you will doubtless arrive at your own answers as your personal philosophy develops. This is just the beginning of developing that philosophy. It starts with questioning your experience of education to date, and striving for something which is more suitable for your child.

Arrange to see other schools. Even if you know you cannot afford private education or are opposed to the system, it does no harm to see what is on offer. Information always helps to formulate your own ideas about what is, and what is not, desirable for your child.

Ask questions about the school's policies on reading, writing and basic skills, and the teaching of those subjects. What are the religious studies policies of the school? What system of rewards and punishments is in operation? What is expected of you, the parent, if your child should come to this school? What is it going to cost you? As well as a uniform and PE kit, some schools charge for books and equipment, hire of musical instruments, and lunches.

If possible, visit when the school is open - there is little to be gained from being shown round an empty building. Note how the children behave, the size of the classes, the quality of the work on display, and whether it is the children's own work or the product of copying an adult's model. Ask yourself whether the display is for the children's benefit, or has it been exhibited to impress adults? Is it visible to children or high up on the wall?

Consider the access to open spaces which the children have and the diversity of the curriculum offered. Check safety and security aspects.

What is the child:adult ratio? Ask if the children have ample opportunity to use facilities; the computer may be kept in a cupboard, or one machine could be shared between fifteen children, for example. Paints and paper should be freely available in the classrooms, you might see sand and water in primary classes. Are the resources actually being used?

How are the tables arranged - in rows or in groups? Look at the extent to which children are encouraged to interact with each other through talking and working together.

Try to take the opportunity to have a look in the lavatories. Are they clean and well cared for? What, if any, restrictions are there upon children who wish to use the lavatory during lesson time? It may seem a strange thing to suggest, but personal experience has shown that much can be learnt from school lavatories as to the ethos and education offered in the school.

View the school critically, listen to what is said to you and to what is going on in the building as you are shown round. If possible, listen to the children. Observe what happens at break times, before and after school and in the playground, and try to get some feedback from parents of children attending the school. The local sweet shop can be a useful source of information. Engage the shopkeeper in informal conversation - his opinion of the children at the school may tell you another side of the story! Schools are an integral part of the community. Their influence extends beyond the boundary fence.

Look at some other types of school, like Montessori, or the Waldorf schools which operate on the philosophies of Rudolf Steiner. Each one is different and the approach to learning within that system is very different from that used in state schools and conventional schooling. Again, be critical. Do not be taken in by the initial impression - find out about the thinking behind the education on offer and take your time to reflect upon it and discuss it within the context of your own family. Some schools expect the entire family to subscribe to the learning system which they operate - is your family prepared to alter their life style to the extent of changing your diet, disposing of the TV set etc. for the sake of your child attending that particular school?

A few specific points:

- Do speak to people other than the staff

- Do watch and listen to the children, both in and out of school.

- Do note the number and frequency of displayed rules, no matter how they have been disguised. Displaying a charter does not make it happen!

- Do not be 'wowed' by displays which look attractive but turn out to be little more than a teacher-made, computer generated summaries of the Literacy Hour, or posters displaying spellings, grammar or times-tables. How much of this is actually the children's own work?

- Do not be put off asking searching questions of the staff. Use the information gathered on visits to help you sort out your own educational agenda, and if necessary, go back to a school and ask for clarification on points which you have missed.

Above all, when considering other schools ask yourself, "Is this a place where my child could be happy and learn? Would they be happy to come here every day?" On this occasion, by all means listen to your child's opinion but bear in mind that schools are attractive places to children, and first impressions may not give a true picture to your child. Unless you take to crawling round a school on hands and knees you will not get the same impression of the place as your child. He will see the boxes of toys, the faces of the other children, the furniture and all the usual trappings of school at his level. It is a place made for people his size, hopefully full of colour and interest and things to be explored. Not until he arrives on Day 1 will he realise that access to all these things is restricted.

It is your job to sort out the messages which schools of whatever type are conveying to you, and your prerogative as a responsible parent to pull rank on this occasion and make the final decision as to whether or not your child should attend the school.

Other Options

Until very recently, school or home was the stark choice - there was nothing in between. Now some real alternatives to both are appearing in the UK in the form of open learning centres. These vary in shape and size, although by school standards all of them are small, operating on a human scale, like extended family units. They are run in private houses, church halls, old school buildings, even converted garages, and provide children with the kind of education which is simply not available in the schools. Often these learning centres have grown from groups of home-educating parents who have grouped together to share resources.

Human Scale Education have, for many years worked to promote small schools and flexi-schooling options. The small schools movement started back in the 1970s with the foundation of the small school at Hartland in Devon, and has grown from that initiative. There are small schools all over the country now. Contact Human Scale Education for details (see resources).

Learning centres are beginning to appear all over the UK and their numbers are growing rapidly. In 1997, Education Now established the Centre for Personalised Education (CPE) - a registered charity which serves as an umbrella under which all the member learning centres can operate. The CPE organises conferences, workshops and discussion group sessions for the members, allowing them the opportunity to meet and learn from each other. Already these tiny new alternatives to school can make use of networking through CPE, using Internet technology. The vision of the future is a time when each centre will be linked by video conferencing facilities, allowing regular personal contact with other centres across the UK without time consuming and expensive travel. Children too could use such links - many children at home already use the e-mail to contact other home-educated friends, share news and information. The virtual school is here!

Because open learning centres are new and small they are not easy to locate. CPE has a list of all its members, and can be contacted for information. New initiatives are appearing all the time, so if a small school or open learning centre might provide a solution for your school problem, contact CPE or Human Scale Education (HSE) for more information on the resources available. Alternatively, band together with other like-minded families and start a project off for yourself. HSE run regular courses for people who are interested in doing this, and CPE will give advice and support anyone interested in setting up an open learning centre, no matter how modest or in what form.

Not all traditional schools are bad news, however. Indeed, there are many caring dedicated teachers and well-behaved, eager young people who are keen to do well within the school system. Even within one family it is not uncommon to find that school suits one child well, they are happy in school and thrive, while a sibling may be terrified of the thought of school and be very happy to learn at home.

To school or not to school has to be a decision made for and at least partially by the individual child. Knowing that there is a choice is sometimes enough to make traditional school bearable if not attractive.

 There is a choice

Chapter Three

Deciding To Take Your Child Out Of School

You pay more for your schooling than your learning is worth.

English Proverb

Why Home-Educate?

Twenty years ago, only about twenty families in Britain were known to have chosen to educate their children in this way, defined by the Education Act 1944 as 'education otherwise than at school'. The present true figure is unknown but it is estimated that now as many as fifty thousand children are educated at home with their parents in the role of tutors. As home education is given more press and media coverage, and dissatisfaction with the school system grows, the number of home educators continues to rise at a steady rate - LEAs expect to hear of a new home-educating family on average once a fortnight. Who does it?

Anyone can opt to teach their own children. No formal teaching or child-care qualifications are required, and no specialist facilities need be available. Successful home educators come from all walks of life, social classes, races and creeds.

As a parent in England or Wales you do not need to obtain any permission from any authority, or to prove to anyone that you are capable of educating your own child. Scottish law is different and authorisation must be sought from the relevant authority.

The misconceptions surrounding home education are widespread, and they extend into the teaching profession and even some Local Education Authorities. As home educators are still very much in the minority it is as well to be certain of your rights as a parent and be prepared to stand up for those rights if and when necessary.

Every year the national press carries features on young children who have passed advanced external examinations or been offered places at university. Many of these children have been home-educated for at least part of their lives - a testimony to the academic successes which are possible through home education.

Roland Meighan, former Special Professor of Education at the University of Nottingham, has studied home education for over twenty years and can be counted amongst the leading authorities on the subject. He works tirelessly to promote personalised learning, basing his arguments upon the evidence from the home educators which he has amassed. Prof. Meighan identifies at least three different kinds of home education:-

- *Parents who want an academic form of education for their children and decide that they can achieve this better at home than at school*

- *Parents who have unhappy or unsuccessful children at school and decide to improve things by home education. They have always been successful in effecting such an improvement in the hundreds of cases I have seen.*

- *Parents who want a different form of education e.g. autonomous, self-directed learning or self-sufficiency skills and know that schools do not provide it so they will have to do it themselves.*

...Home education has been shown to work in all three categories.

But desire for academic excellence is far from being the only reason to opt for a home education for your child:

- The instances of 'new-age bullying' - that is, bullying of a particularly severe kind - is becoming more frequent, even in groups of very young children.

- Stress affects all ages and social groups. Children suffer as much if not more than adults from being in a stressful environment. For many children, school can be intolerably stressful.

- Large classes, low morale amongst teaching staff, pressure to 'succeed' by passing examinations and the effects of financial cutbacks in the education budget have contributed to the present unhappy climate in many of our schools at the present time.

- The constraints of the school timetable, in particular since the advent of the National Curriculum, are a cause for concern for some families. Many who choose to home-educate do so on the grounds that their children are not able to receive what parents consider to be a full and balanced education in school.

There is a significant body of home educators who choose to educate children themselves because they are dissatisfied with the quality of religious and moral education in schools. Children who do not meet the requirements of the National Curriculum's age/stage development testing and assessment also give parents cause to doubt the wisdom of continuing with education within the school system. At home children can be treated as individuals, rather than as part of a group known as Key Stage 1/2/3 or Year 6/7/8 etc. - meaningless terms which bear no relation to the age of the child! Under the school regime, the bright children are at as much of a disadvantage as those who find learning more difficult.

Teachers are required to both educate and control very large numbers of children in a confined space and with limited resources. In order to achieve this, children cannot be treated as individuals - there simply is not time in a school day or space in an already crowded classroom. By grouping children together, some order can be achieved, and some kind of educational activity take place. It may not be an ideal education, it may not be the best for every child, but it eases the teacher's job of crowd controller. The needs of the individual can easily be overlooked in a classroom, and being bright can present as many problems as having difficulty with the work given. Often it is the brighter children who are the most disruptive when boredom paves the way for antisocial behaviour.

Doing well in academic study at school may seriously affect your social life.

Students want to look the same, dress in the same way, behave in the same way, and achieve similar results in public examinations. Who wants to be a 'clever clogs' and have no friends?

Educationally advanced children present as much of a problem to a school as educationally challenged children. If either is to achieve their best potential, some investment of time and therefore money must be made in providing extra tuition. Extra resources and space must be found in which these people are to work.

Their problems must be identified and properly diagnosed. The tasks required of them must be compatible with the standardised curriculum and testing procedures.

In the present educational climate in the UK we see another problem - that of the growing number of children who have been expelled, permanently excluded from school or have no place at a local school in areas where the schools are over-subscribed. There are also schools which are deemed to be 'failing' and are threatened with closure. Children are faced with the prospect of making long journeys to and from school, often at the expense of their families, while parents are being expected to take more and more responsibility for their child's education through the introduction of home-school contracts.

The ability of schools to hire and fire, to choose pupils who they want and to exclude those who they do not is effectively creating a school-less class - a significant number of children who have nowhere to go for an education. They are neither truants nor home-educated and, unless there are good medical grounds, home tuition will not be provided by the Local Authority. Such children join the ranks of the Great Uneducated, along with the homeless and unemployed, a feature of modern society in the UK.

Whatever the reason for withdrawing a child from school, the decision to do so, and to take responsibility for a child's education upon oneself is never an easy one to take. It takes courage to take on the mantle of educator, especially when the alternative is such a vast institution, established and respected as the 'best' place for children to learn. School is so ingrained in society as desirable and good that it seems incomprehensible to reject it, and yet more and more families are doing just that.

Reluctant Home Educators

The research which has been published by groups like Education Now, Educational Heretics Press and Education Otherwise suggests that the majority of home-educating families have taken the decision to do so reluctantly. Having made that decision and successfully embarked upon an individual programme of home education, few would choose to return to school. Parents quickly find that the advantages of flexible, personalised learning at home far outweigh the disadvantages.

Most home educators have made the decision to educate their own children because schooling has failed - or would fail - their children in some way. Their prime concern is for the well-being of their children, and feel that they have no choice but to home-educate when things go badly wrong at school.

When the school system is no longer a viable proposition, and in the absence of any alternative to school, home education is frequently the only choice available. There are a number of typical scenarios for this state.

Some Different Kinds Of Home Educators

Temporary Home Educators

For some, home education may be a transitory solution to a problem in school. Home education is taken on as a temporary measure, and it is always intended that the child should return to school when the particular problem has been resolved. Sometimes the choice of home education is temporary because of the financial burden which it places upon a family - a significant number of families notice that the biggest immediate difference home education makes to them is the loss of one income. Yet very few seem to regret this loss, finding that the benefits of home education far outweigh the disadvantage of a loss of one income. Indeed, some families would rather continue home-educating and live well below the defined poverty limit rather than return children to school. Parents remark on children being physically healthier since leaving school, happier and learning more. The loss of salary is more than balanced out by the peace of mind.

Virtually no one regretted the loss of income or status. Many parents indicated that they had learned or were learning a great deal that was positive from the experience, in terms of personal development and close involvement with their children...
Alan Thomas, Educating Children At Home

Home education does not work for everyone. No shame should be felt by parents or children for whom this is the case. In our experience, the main factor in the success of home education is enjoyment, on the part of all who are involved.

Converted Home Educators

Some home educators who leave the school system will never return. Home education is often entered into reluctantly when problems arise within school, but in many cases it is so successful that neither children or parents wish to return to the school system. Such families often become the most ardent supporters of the home education option

The thought of her returning to school sickens me...she's learnt so much, come on so well in the last year.
Home ed. parent faced with prospect of the child returning to school in the event of family difficulties

Committed Home Educators

There are some whose parents make the conscious decision never to send their child to school in the first place. These home educators are often influenced by their own moral values or religious faith. There may be no suitable alternative school provision available in the area of their home, or they may be committed to home education from the onset. There is a large community of home educators in religious groups.

Perhaps you can identify with one of these broad groups. If so, by identifying your reasons for opting to home-educate your personal philosophy may become clearer. If you see yourself as a temporary home educator it may be that the content of the National Curriculum is important to you and will have some bearing upon what you hope to achieve with your children at home. If, however, you believe that your children are not being allowed to develop to their fullest potential, and find the National Curriculum a constraint of the school system which you could well do without, your approach to learning will be quite different. It could be that you fall into the last category of committed home educators who have chosen this path because of the profound influence of your faith or dedication to an alternative lifestyle, in which case priorities may be different again. For some, the structure of a curriculum will be very necessary. For others, any form of structure in learning will be abhorrent.

Only you can decide. Whatever your reasons for choosing to home-educate your decision will have an effect upon yourselves, your family and all whom you come into contact with.

Are There Other Home Educators In My Area?

Yes, there are certain to be! The popularity of home education has increased so much in the last ten years, and is continuing to do so at a steady rate, that it is unlikely that there is any corner of the British Isles where there are no home-educating families in residence. Of course, if you live in a centre of population you are more likely to be nearby to other home-educating people than if your home is in rural Wales or Scotland. Home education seems to be taken up by all kinds of people from all walks of life. There do seem to be pockets where it is more prevalent than in other places, either because of problems associated with a particular school or LEA, or because there is a thriving 'alternative' culture.

Joining a support group will give you access to a contact list of home educators, and many towns now have some form of learning centre or voluntary support group where families can meet others, share resources and ideas. Do remember that you can join support groups *before* you make your final decision. Use contact lists to talk over your concerns with people who have probably been there themselves. If you have Internet access you will find there are groups that can be joined which are extremely useful for gathering information and discussing issues.

How Home Education Will Affect You

The decision to home-educate is a major one. It will affect the entire family, including extended family members who may live some distance away and whom you rarely see. In home-educating we find that we not only educate our children, but other members of our family, friends and neighbours, and strangers who we meet in the shops or the street. In constantly having to take the responsibility, answer the questions and explain the rationale of home education, we are learning the whole time.

To take on the education of one's own children requires patience and devotion to the task. It is not for the faint-hearted or the house-proud. For example, the papier maché castle which the children are making does not stay in the classroom at the end of the day, but will probably be adorning your sideboard for several weeks in various stages of construction. Unless you have a house large enough to accommodate a 'classroom' and wish to work in this way, the whole family will have to live with the children's work displayed around them.

Glue will be spilt on the floor, painted fingers will touch the walls and glitter dust will get on to the sofa. Perhaps people who happily continue with home education have different priorities from those who send children to school, no matter how intolerable the schooling becomes. One mother of a home-educated family summed up her attitude in this way, "The house is always untidy, but everyone is well and happy." If you cannot tolerate some untidiness, home education is probably not for you.

To take on this job of home educator you do need certain qualities. Some of them may have already become apparent:

1. You will need determination, and a willingness to fight against the odds for what you believe is right for your child.

2. Confidence in your own ability is a must. This may have already been questioned, and it will continue to be no matter how well qualified you become. This is the downside of the job. We all get it at some time or another. It is counteracted with being able to justify your actions, confidence in your own ability and ultimately, faith.

3. You have to be tough. Tough enough to stand up for what you believe is right in the face of 'officials' and critics, perhaps even tough enough to brave out interviews from newspaper reporters or television crews who are looking for a novelty item to fill in on a slow news day. People will ask questions - are you brave enough to give them the answers?

4. You have to be honest - if you do not know an answer (and none of us knows everything) say so, but be prepared to spend time and effort in finding that answer out for yourself.

Knowledge is of two kinds. We know a subject ourselves, or we know where we can find information upon it.
Samuel Johnson - Letter to Lord Chesterfield 1755

5. You have to be nosy. Ask questions, speak to the people who can give the answers you require, keep probing until you get the information you want, and when one line of enquiry reaches a dead end, try a different route.

Action! **Work through this list, considering each point in turn. Discuss the issues raised here with a partner or friend. How many can you tick off with confidence? How many more do you imagine you could tick off in time? Are there any which you cannot identify with?**

If time and effort is given to the education of children at home it is a rewarding, enjoyable experience and an education in itself. Home-educated families develop close bonds and friendships between parents, children and siblings. When home education does not work, it can be a nightmare, with all the members of the family feeling as if the worst long summer holiday from school will go on indefinitely without the advantage of having pleasant weather. When home education works well it can work like a dream. Children make good progress, often well beyond their peer group in school, and are happy and secure. Parents feel that they are doing their best for their children and enjoy the time spent as a family.

> **Action!** Before coming to a final decision, talk about what education means to you and your family. Could you do as well as a school? What sacrifices would need to be made to home-educate? How willing is your child to co-operate and to work at home? What is your relationship with your child like, and would you be able to cope? Who could you call on for help with subjects which may be outside of your knowledge?

Frequently Asked Questions

The likelihood is that you have already come to some kind of decision about education. If you do feel inclined to reject the school version of education, pause for a moment and try this...

Action! Assuming you do not like what schools have on offer, list ten ideals in education, i.e. what do you want an education to provide for your child?

It may be that some of the points on your list are already addressed at school. For instance, you may have written *"I want education to equip my child with the skills he will need for life"*. How are schools already providing this? Work experience? Skills-based lessons like woodwork and metal-work, CDT (craft, design and technology), exposure to Information Technology and training in the use of computers, work in the community?

In the past twenty years, schools have made great efforts to work more closely with industry and to accommodate the demands of parents. Governments have built policies and guidelines into the National Curriculum in an attempt to meet these needs. If, in your opinion, these measures have failed to deliver, be prepared to specify exactly what is wrong, to argue your point and to suggest a remedy which you are able to offer. Critics will cite these points. How will you reply to them?

Action! Try working through your own ten points in this way, listing the arguments for and against the education offered by schools, and considering what they offer, what you could offer and which might be better suited to the needs of your child.

Curiously, it is by talking that we are able to sort out our own thoughts (a point worth remembering when working with children). By being in a position of having to justify your choice to home-educate to others will actually help you to develop your own thoughts, question your decision in a constructive way, and build your own confidence. What follows is a selection of the questions which we have most frequently been asked and the rationale behind the answers we give. The answers are not necessarily 'right' or 'wrong', but based upon our own experience and information at the moment. You may disagree - or at least question our opinions. We hope you do,

---

for they are only opinions, and questioning them will lead you to a clearer understanding of your own criteria of a satisfactory education.

Q. What about the social side?

Whenever we are asked this, our mental response is, *"Excuse me, what social side?"* In our experience, nothing very positive came out of the 'social side' of school for our children. In turn, two of our children went as four-year-olds to school. They left us as children who we had brought up to say 'please' and 'thank-you', to wait their turn and respect the needs of people both younger and older than themselves, to care for their possessions and to care for their environment. On each occasion school sent back a child who was almost unrecognisable in terms of behaviour. He used push and shove as a means of getting his own way. He treated younger siblings with disdain to the point of being unkind, which was a shift in behaviour particularly distressing because of the young children's total inability to comprehend it. He left once treasured toys and books lying where they had been dropped and would walk over or roughly kick any obstacle in his path out of the way. This change in behaviour was alarmingly rapid - within a few days of starting school each child had changed considerably in this respect.

The social side of school also brought our children's complaints of *"so-and-so kicked, so-and-so pushed, so-and-so snatched and wouldn't give back"*. Our children, it seemed, did not have the skills to deal effectively with anti-social behaviour from other children, and as the staff were apparently unable to deal with this either, the children soon learnt to fend for themselves by retaliation tactics which became a 'normal' part of life. School's most effective lesson to our children was to teach them how to fight back. The social side taught them how to use language which we had never heard at home, and it taught them to disregard the values which we had spent five years of devoted parenthood instilling in them. Through the social side of school they learned to mock and tease without mercy, to call names and to take part in team games not through co-operation but in direct and aggressive competition.

Our children did not enjoy the social side of school. Neither did the rest of the family. It is unlikely that we are the only family to experience this kind of change when children start school. Certainly, for every time we hear this question we hear a parent complaining of the bad language or unacceptable behaviour their own children *"picked up at school"*.

> *"'Who is she, anyway?" said Leakey.*
>
> *I shrugged.*
>
> *"She's called Mina."*
>
> *"What school's she at?"*
>
> *"She doesn't go to school."*
>
> *They looked at me. "How's that?" said Leakey.*
>
> *"Plays the wag?" said Coot.*
>
> *"Her mother teaches her," I said.*
>
> *They looked again.*
>
> *"Bloody hell," said Leakey. "I thought you had to go to school."*
>
> *"Imagine it," said Coot.*
>
> *They imagined it for a while.*
>
> *"Lucky sod," said Leakey.*
>
> *"What'll she do for mates, though?" said Coot. "And who'd like to be stuck at home all day?"*
>
> **David Almond, Skellig**

It could be that a home-educated child has greater need of social contact than he will receive day by day. This may be accentuated if he is an only child, living in a remote area. School is not necessarily the only solution, but alternative possibilities should be considered.

Action! Make some critical evaluation of the social side of school in your experience. How has it affected your child? What social activities do they enjoy? What do they dislike/fear? How will you make some provision for your child to meet and learn with other children if you home-educate?

Q. What about sex education?

Sex education is part of the school curriculum, and delivered as a package of lessons to classes or groups. At home, it is up to you, as parents, when you tell your children about personal relationships and how this information is given. Whatever your feelings on this matter, two things are evident:

i. At home children learn by asking questions. They learn by receiving the amount of information with which they can cope at any given time. By answering their questions honestly and as they arise and giving the extent of the information which you judge appropriate, the child will learn about sex gradually and normally, rather than having the whole story from menstruation to homosexuality potted and delivered in a short space of time and in the company of other children of both sexes.

ii. The children will learn about love as being central to the whole question of sex and sexual relationships. You will have the opportunity to explain the physical and biological side of the process of baby-making in terms of a loving secure relationship. This is sometimes overlooked when sex lessons in school are given by an adult who is a virtual stranger. Any religious aspects regarding sex which you would wish to emphasise are also possible at home, without the confusion which arises from the chatter of schoolchildren 'behind the bike-sheds'.

Teaching sex in school has always been a ticklish subject. After all, it's a very private thing and not everyone wants to talk about it. It puts the teachers in a difficult position. If they appear to know too much or too little about it, it throws up all sorts of speculation about their private lives. And of course, the subject makes people giggle. However, I suppose schools will always feel an obligation to teach it, although I think it's unlikely that there'll ever be an exam in it - not a practical one, anyway!
Peter Corey , Coping With School

Q. What about PE and games?

If they enjoy nothing else in school, many children enjoy PE and Games lessons. Some skills, like swimming and gymnastics, are more effectively taught in a group, as children learn physical skills by copying and through competition. A few children do not enjoy sports at all. Their memories of games invariably include waiting to be picked last for a team, and hearing the groans of mates as they bemoan the fact that you are on their team, perfecting the art of climbing up the walls of the lavatory to avoid detection by the teacher, thus getting out of the hockey lesson, etc.

Home education is challenging if you include team games and gymnastic excellence in your criteria for a full and balanced education. Home educators have effectively opted for a private form of education, so although opportunities for participation in sports and games are available, time must be found to fit these into a busy day, and money is necessary to pay for the use of sports facilities and expert coaching. On the other hand, not having to attend school at the same time as other children leaves plenty of space when swimming pools are empty and parks and leisure centres are quiet. We have found that the local horse riding centre are only too pleased to accommodate our family plus home-educated friends for private riding lessons during the day. In the winter this is particularly useful, as we would otherwise be restricted to the hours of daylight at the weekends. Home education also opens up opportunities to try sports which would not usually form part of the school curriculum, and which demand self-discipline and self-evaluation rather than competitive team events. One of our sons has taken up archery, and very much enjoys going to an archery club one or two evenings a week. The opportunity is there for him to take part in tournaments with the club, and he mixes with people of all ages who share his interest.

Another of our children has recently taken up rock climbing. He attends weekly sessions at an indoor climbing school as part of a group of five children. They learn co-operative skills for real - one is very dependent on a partner who is holding the other end of the rope when you are thirty feet above the ground. The cost of taking part is not prohibitive, but the timing of the activities, in the evenings and afternoons would have been impossible for us to accommodate with a full school day and homework.

Our own children take part in team sports and activities and have learnt to work as part of a team rather than as competitors. Although this approach suits their nature, it may not suit your family. Only you can decide.

Q. How's it going, then?

(translated as: "How do you know the children are learning anything?")

We are never certain what the required or expected answer to this question is. Do people want us to say, *"Oh, he's not doing so well on his maths"*, or *"she has a reading age of fourteen and three quarters, and she's only six"* or perhaps *"the kids are fine, but I've got piles of marking to do and I'm going round the bend with being at home with them all day"*. We have come to believe that this is really a gambit question - what they actually want to know is *What is going on in that house? Are they doing lessons all day? The children seem well, happy and intelligent enough, but are they up to passing the SATS which my lot have just been put through?* Maybe we disappoint with our answer which is invariably a rather puzzled, *"Fine, thank you."*

We operate under the premise that *"the pig doesn't get bigger by weighing it"*, and the child does not learn any more by testing. Should you feel the need to test a child, reading tests, IQ tests, SATS papers and sample GCSE tests are available from the High Street book shops. Home-educated children can enter selection examinations for Grammar schools (if your LEA still has them), and the standard SATS tests as taken by schoolchildren are obtainable from the DfEE. Sometimes, a measure of success in external standardised examinations is interesting, but probably more from your point of view as a parent than to the child.

A Pig

For a teacher, it is not possible to know whether what has been attempted in any day's work has been successful. A child may appear to learn the name and sound of a letter one day and have completely forgotten it the next. Or he may appear to 'know his tables', recite them and score well in a test, but he has no idea how to use this information; he could easily have forgotten them altogether within a few months. The importance has been emphasised of seeing one's own work as only one small part of a much larger process. The car factory worker whose job it is to stick, say, the boot rubber on each new vehicle is taken on a tour of the factory to view the whole process from of car manufacture, from sheet metal to driving off the conveyor belt. He is able to see how his job fits into the rest of the process, and presumably he goes home a happy man.

Teachers never have this opportunity. The children are presented as a class, and although each child is at a different stage of development, all are bundled together for the teacher to do her best with during the school year. She may regroup, rearrange, pay more attention to some than to others, but she must get through the prescribed National Curriculum during that time. She must strive to develop a relationship with each child which is based upon trust and friendship, and in the course of doing that she gets to know the family too. At the end of the year, the children leave the care of that teacher, and apart from a nod of recognition as they pass in the corridor, nothing remains of the teacher/child relationship which had once been so close. A teacher may hear how someone has at last learnt to swim, but still cannot catch a ball - how someone else is better at maths than he was, but still struggling - this is the stuff of staff room gossip, but as a teacher you never really know if you have taught a child anything. One can never be sure. Unless you are fortunate enough to met an ex-pupil in later life and they make a point of mentioning something they know they learned from you, teachers go through their lives wondering if they are any good at their job, or if they are simply keeping the crowd under control.

Parents on the other hand, stand a much better chance of seeing the whole process through from start to finish, from conception to the day when your baby boy or girl is a grown man or woman, a happy and well-balanced adult (we hope!)

Q. What About Secondary Level And GCSEs?

There is no reason why home education cannot continue through secondary school level and include GCSE study. The break between Primary and Secondary school accentuates the change in education at the age of 11, but there is no sound educational reason for adopting a radical change at this time. Older children should be able to concentrate for longer periods and may be expected to have a more extensive curriculum than young children, perhaps incorporating formal study of languages, music or specialist sport, but otherwise there is no need to make any drastic changes to the way in which you work when a child reaches the 'magic' age of 11.

It is, in fact, nothing short of a miracle that the modern methods of instruction have not yet entirely strangled the holy curiosity of inquiry.
Albert Einstein

If a child intends to sit GCSEs, this can be done at any time. As home educators you will have to pay a fee for the examination, but there are no age limits. We are led to believe some LEAs have provision for ALL children to sit GCSE Maths and English free of charge. It may be worth enquiring as to whether such a scheme exists in your area. It is not uncommon for children as young as ten to pass a GCSE, and as a parent, you too could take a GCSE if you wanted to.

Conversely, there is no reason why GCSEs and A-levels should not be taken years after the normal age. As the freedom enjoyed by home educators becomes apparent, the arbitrary rules and regulations which have become the accepted way of life in a society of institutions vanish. Everything is possible.

The local library should have details of Open Learning courses in your area, and these will include the GCSE syllabuses. Further Education colleges and the Open College may also have details of distance learning and part-time courses. The Internet is a rich seam of information on external examination courses and syllabuses. Now it is free it is becoming increasingly accessible to all, and well worth considering as a resource for home educators.

The point which arises from any discussion about home education and GCSE/A-level examinations is what are these examinations for? What do they prove? What use are they? The GCSE (General Certificate of Secondary Education) proves that a child has attended a secondary school and learnt enough about both a given subject and examination technique to pass an examination. Reaching this stage will give some indication to a prospective employer of... well, what, exactly? That this particular young person has been able to stick school for eleven years and, moreover, has knuckled under to the demands of the system well enough to pass the exam. In short, they have learnt that if someone in authority says 'frog' they jump, through a hoop if necessary. Do these qualifications tell us anything about initiative, creative thought, individual expression, common sense or ability to survive, let alone politeness, awareness of the needs of others or concern for fellow man?

> **Action!** Define your own ideas regarding the need for GCSEs. If your child is, like many, leaving school as a teenager, pre GCSE, or is worried or under pressure from the GCSE syllabus, consider ways in which the stress might be averted or eliminated.

A-levels are designed as pre-entrance examinations for further education. Three decent passes are normally required for University entrance, and in the normal course of events, students who have achieved good passes at GCSE are encouraged to study for a further two years for A-levels. A-levels differ from GCSE in as much as some interpretation of the information given on any subject is required. To pass A-levels demands a similar amount of input on behalf of the student as a degree, but GCSE is not a pre-requisite for an A-level course.

The lesson here is that GCSEs and A-levels can be taken at any time. You will have to pay for them yourself or find an establishment which will enrol you as a student. If you do want a higher qualification, then consider the following:-

Option 1 -   Attend a conventional university, assuming you have at least the legal minimum A-level results. Follow one of a handful of courses you are qualified to by your A-level results. Maybe realise that it is now too late to change direction very far - you may very well have chosen your career path for the rest of your life at the age of sixteen. Emerge three years later with a certificate, a huge debt from the student loan system and no real work experience to help you get that all-important first job.

Option 2 -   Take a straightforward job, selling burgers or stacking supermarket shelves for example. Register with the Open University for courses that interest you that year - no GCSEs or A-levels required for this. Depending on the pace at which you want to take your degree, emerge between three and twelve years later with a certificate, work experience that proves a lot to a potential employer and will have given you the opportunity to pay your way as you go, and a degree that reflects your possibly changing interests.

Of course, this is not a guaranteed path for success in staying employed - there is no such assurance for anybody. Many people would consider the experience of the university campus as being crucial to further education. But do consider the Open University option - flexibility and an open mind to education are as important at the student's age of eighteen as they were when he was five.

Degrees from the Open University can be obtained in three years of full-time study. Students have to pay for their courses of study, but they do at any university now, anyway. The choice of subjects is very wide-ranging and can be mixed and matched according to personal interest. Anyone who has considered an OU course will be aware of the tremendous demands which the OU puts upon students in terms of workload, making the prized degrees very well accepted and respected in academic circles.

The Open University is available to anyone over the age of eighteen. With special approval there have been a few cases of younger entry - you would have to contact the nearest regional director to get more details about this. In the first place call the Open University at the address given at the end of this book.

Even if the child is too young for registration there is no reason why a parent cannot register, work through the credits themselves and involve their home-educated children in the same course work at home, learning together. It is a common phenomenon amongst home educators that their own enthusiasm for learning is rekindled; parents often want to study alongside their children.

A flexible approach to learning applies throughout the whole of the student's life.

All this may sound radical and far-fetched, but give it a moment's thought. We have. Why should our children bother with the stresses of GCSE if they can get a degree without them? The OU does not require as much as a cycling proficiency certificate for entrance to its courses.

In a similar way, home educators have been using the Adult Learning programmes which run at local schools and colleges for years. These are only open to adults as part of a government backed scheme (children under 15 cannot normally register), but there is no reason why a parent should not register on a course, even take a well-behaved, quiet youngster along to the lectures if a childminder is not available, and share the information and coursework with the home-educated child. This really is killing two birds with one stone - the parent can get a qualification which they may not have had, and the experience extends the child's education at home.

Schools no longer have the monopoly on learning or examinations. The fact that we think they do is a stumbling block of our society.

Q. Don't you have to have teaching qualifications?

followed by, "It's OK for you, you're a teacher. I wouldn't know where to begin."

The answers are: NO, you do not need any qualifications at all to teach your own children at home, and YES, I trained as a teacher and taught in schools before teaching my own children.

Incidentally, it is interesting to see the percentage of known home educators who do have teaching qualifications and experience. Maybe this is because trained teachers have the confidence and knowledge of resources needed. If this is the case then we trust that this book will be an apt substitute. We suspect that the high incidence of qualified home educators tells us something about the quality of education given in schools, however.

School teaching is very different from home education, and teaching other people's children is very different from teaching your own. Experience in the teaching profession does give skills but, more than anything else, the confidence to take on the job of home-educating, especially when dealing with criticism and answering questions from people in positions of authority. It also helps to know of the existence of certain teaching materials and where to obtain them. None of this information is unavailable to an interested parent, however. Experience and confidence, however, cannot be purchased or taught, and will only be acquired with time in home education and contact with other people in the same job. (see the list of support groups at the end of this book).

One can begin by considering how much a child knew before he went to school, who taught him and how. Did he learn to walk by formal lessons? How did he learn to feed, dress and undress himself? And who was it who taught him the most difficult thing he is ever likely to master - Language? How did he learn that - by careful study with books, paper and pens? Of course not!

 However few qualifications you have yourself, you still have both the right and the ability to teach your child at home.

Q. Aren't you over-protecting your children?

"You are over-protecting your children. Kids won't be able to cope with the tough adult world if they haven't learnt to be tough in school."

Roger and Tina Rich-Smith (A Delightful Happening, Learning From Home Education) saw this question as linked to the common accusation of home educators depriving their children of social contact with friends of their own age. Their answer to this criticism is thus:

...If we take parenting seriously then we must take society seriously. Children do not exist in a vacuum and it is entirely inappropriate to wrap them in cotton wool. A well thought out home education (and quite probably any home education) provides many opportunities for social contact.

Few people go through life without encountering some problems in relationships, perhaps with neighbours, friends, relations, partners, the local council, the postman... We are no exception to that. At home all day, our children inevitably witness our squabbles, are there to see how we deal with disputes in shops, or how we respond when the council sends out another tax bill in error. They learn by our example how to deal with the world, which course of action is appropriate to any situation, and they learn about the levels of stress different conflicts generate. They have learnt by observation, questioning, testing and discussion what problems can get shrugged off and dismissed as silly, and which deserve more serious attention and action.

What they do not witness is fighting or bullying. So the answer to this criticism is that, through example, the children learn to deal with a tough old world in a responsible adult way. They have a healthily cautious attitude towards strangers but generally trusting, loving people who would go out of their way to give assistance when needed. They have no concept of fighting or violence beyond what they have seen on television, and therefore they do not associate violence with reality. It is out of the bounds of their experience. Thankfully, it is out of the bounds of ours too. Neither of us as parents have much idea of being streetwise beyond common sense, and while we would naturally defend our children to the bitter end we would not seek a fight or set out wilfully to offend anyone.

It may be that some people take advantage of our children's honesty and good nature. We have been conned on more than one occasion by beggars, friends and financial institutions. To them, *good luck* and may the perpetrators of the crime find happiness with whatever they have gained at our expense. We would rather bring up our children to be pleasant people who are conned once in a while than hard-nosed streetwise kids whom people move away from rather than towards. Our belief is that our gains will be the greater in the end.

Disadvantages Of Home Education

The decision to home-educate should never be taken lightly. The advantages of home education over schooling are numerous, as home educators are quick to point out. But there are factors involved which some may see as disadvantages, and both sides of the argument must be explored and the effects on the whole family considered before taking any irrevocable steps in the direction of home education.

First, in some authorities the schools are over-subscribed. That means that there are insufficient places in the schools to meet the demand from the children in that area. If you withdraw your child from a school in such an area there may be no guarantee that you will be able to get him back into the system in a local school if home education does not work for you.

Secondly, choosing to home-educate is not a cheap option. You may save transport costs to and from school, dinner money, school uniform, and the regular requests for donations and financial support, but home education is effectively the same as choosing private education and you can expect no financial help to be forthcoming from the LEA. All the expenses incurred for books, equipment, examination fees, visits, etc. will have to be met by you.

Thirdly, effective home education requires devotion to the point of education becoming a way of life for the whole family. One adult must be with the child all the time and this can mean giving up a job and the income which goes with it.

When your child has gone to bed and you think you might like to put your feet up, it is really time to write up your diary (see page 96) and plan for tomorrow. This kind of devotion is a must, at least until you are absolutely established as a home educator.

Home education can be a joy if it suits you and your family. It can be a nightmare if it does not, so please think carefully before withdrawing your child from school. Try working through the school holidays or when the child is not attending school. Talk to other home educators about their experiences and talk to your child about the idea of working at home. We cannot emphasise too strongly the need for full and honest reflection and self-analysis prior to taking the enormous step towards home education. As ever, our main concern in writing this book is the well-being of children. The worst-case scenario for an unhappy child is constant moving from one type of school to home and then back to school again. Hopefully, by taking time to work through this chapter thoroughly some of your questions about home education in relation to your own personal situation will be answered before you take the final decision. This chapter explores the arguments for and against home education and presents the case as we see it. If you are considering home-educating you will need to have a clear idea of your aims, to have worked out a philosophy and to be able to justify your choice.

Pros And Cons Of Home Education

For	Against
i. The children are happy, secure and working to their own ability. The causes of stress in school are removed.	i. It may prove very difficult for the child to return to school.
ii. They are able to extend and develop their individual skills and interests.	ii. Only one parent can work, so the family income is restricted.
iii. Parents have the option of instilling their own principles, whether educational, moral or religious.	iii. In some situations the child may be rather isolated. It is necessary to make an effort to ensure that the children mix with others in their peer group. That, itself can bring problems.
iv. The children learn to co-operate and work together, despite age differences.	iv. Free time is limited, as the children are with the family all of the time.
v. The family operates as a unit, rather than everyone going their separate ways each day and having little in common.	v. The house is full of the children's work, it is seldom tidy and needs frequent redecorating.
vi. The children have been brought up with one set of rules about behaviour and manners, and are therefore well-mannered and polite.	vi. Organising and recording the work for the children is time consuming and needs to be done regularly every day.
vii. The children are confident in the company of people of all ages, and not intimidated by adults who are in positions of authority.	vii. All books, stationery and apparatus has to be bought, as does any specialist tuition.
viii. The children have developed skills of	viii. It can cause friction within the extended family and circle of friends and

research and the ability to work at their own pace and on their own. They take on more responsibility and are therefore more able to cope responsibly later on.

ix. 'Holidays' and 'term times' are very fluid concepts. Home-educating families work whenever it is most appropriate. Families are not tied to school holidays and can go where they want, when they want, avoiding crowds and inflated prices.

x. Parents have few problems with discipline because the children are seldom, if ever, bored.

xi. Children learn more of life than they would at school. Learning about real life in a school is like learning to swim without getting wet.

xii. It is interesting. We learn alongside the children.

xiii. We have maintained a close relationship with our children which disappeared in the short time that the eldest attended school.

xiv. Interest in our children's education has been a significant factor in us furthering our own education.

acquaintances, when those people are critical of home education.

ix. Stress within the family can be introduced from LEA inspections.

Naturally, our list of advantages is considerably greater than our list of disadvantages. Use this list as a starting point when considering your own family, and add to it. If the disadvantages immediately outweigh the advantages, then maybe home education is not for you.

Chapter Four

Developing A Philosophy

*New opinions are always suspected, and usually opposed, without
any other reason but because they are not already common.*

John Locke, Essay Concerning Human Understanding

Justifying Your Decision

Choosing to home-educate means choosing a little known,
misunderstood mode of education in preference to a well-
established, socially accepted norm - school. Whether or not
you like it, people will question your decision, and you will be
put 'on the spot' and expected to come up with some good
answers. You will probably be criticised, perhaps by close
friends or family. You will almost certainly be asked to justify
your methods in some detail by the local authority, in writing in
response to their enquiries and possibly in an interview. This
may all sound very alarming, especially if you have no
experience or knowledge of educational philosophy or jargon. It
is an issue needs to be addressed by home educators,
however, ideally before any final decisions are made.

To use simple terms, why have you made this choice, and how
are you going to put it into practice? People who question your
decision are seeking assurance that you have thought it all
through. Sometimes, in questioning you, they are questioning
their own philosophy - and quite often, as far as the education
of their children is concerned, they find they do not have one!

---

 *A philosophy need not be as grand as it sounds.
The definition of the word 'philosophy' as given in
Chambers Dictionary is...*

**"...the pursuit of wisdom and knowledge; the
principals underlying any department of
knowledge: reasoning;..."**

*...and most interestingly in relation to home
educators in certain tricky situations...*

"calmness of temper..."!

In many cases it is a small, almost insignificant, incident which provides the catalyst for the path to home education - detention for wearing a coat of the wrong colour, suspension for answering a teacher in what has been construed as a rude manner, a misunderstanding over an incident with another pupil...

Such incidents in isolation seldom give parents reason to withdraw a child from school, but when the last straw breaks the camel's back questions arise about many of the practices within the school. Once questions have arisen beyond a certain level, the family is likely to become aware of many unresolved grievances that have built up over a period. It becomes clear that the relationship between the child, parents and school is untenable, and the child is deregistered. In such cases it may be easy to misconstrue the family's motives as taking drastic action; comments from neighbours or fellow pupils like, *they took him out because they wouldn't buy him a black coat* or *he was rude to Mr. Smith* will place the blame firmly upon the family who have, in fact, been the victims. If you are in this last straw situation, and you have removed your child from a school, try to look at the overall picture and answer a few questions for yourselves, so that you are in a better position to set records straight with whosoever may enquire.

Action! Why have you decided to home educate? Is it because: a) the child has failed in school? b) the school has failed the child - academically, socially or both? If the latter, have you made every effort to resolve the situation? Is your grievance with the one school, or are you now questioning the school system? Would the situation be different at any other school?

It may be unfair and unwise to criticise a particular school, especially if you live nearby to it or in its catchment area. Many parents will not be in a position to consider an alternative. They may also take exception to your child's removal from the school, interpreting it as a criticism of their decision to stick with schooling. It is also unfair on the school; many professionals in education are as unhappy and as doubtful of the system as you are, but are powerless to make any effective changes. Unlike individual families they are unable to walk away or to change the parts of the system which they do not like. They have to exist from day to day, making the best of a failed system.

"We tried school and gave it a fair chance. We tried to resolve the problems which arose. School didn't suit our children, and they didn't suit school". This was our standard answer, and it was enough to satisfy casual enquirers. In the end perhaps the only attitude is to agree to differ with the school system, say as little as possible in day-to-day conversations and put the unhappy episode behind you. Home educators are under no obligation to justify their decision to the LEA, to the school or to any other official body; home education is your right. There will be occasions, however, when people will ask and an answer of some kind is required. Be prepared to give that answer.

"There Are More Questions Than Answers

... and the more I find out the less I know" - Johnny Nash

In removing your child from school, or not starting off at school, you have rejected one system, but what will you put in its place? At first the answer may be 'don't know' and the action will be 'nothing at all' - an acceptable and even desirable solution for a while (see Deschooling, page 103). Parents need deschooling too, and philosophies take time to develop. Remember that the LEA will have to allow you time to get going with home education.

Having questioned, have the confidence to carry on. Find out more about alternative learning systems and how children learn. Listen to your child, his anger and his needs, and talk to other members of your close family. Through these actions you will be able to find the answers to some of your questions, and the cycle of planning, action, observation and reflection will begin. Time is a necessary ingredient in this recipe for successful home education. Your ideas and philosophies will change with time. Keep a record of your thoughts and answers to the exercises in this chapter and re-evaluate them in six months or a year in the light of your experiences of home education. If you have only recently deregistered your child or are considering doing so, it may be difficult to define the answers to some of these questions at the moment. Your thoughts will change as you find out more about your child and his individual learning strategy. Information about alternative ways of learning to schooling will force you to change your opinions, ask further questions and find your own answers. You are learning too, and this is only the beginning...

> **Action!** "Learning should not be fun all the time"; "Children need discipline. That is what school gives"; "If they only learn what they want to learn, they will miss out on a lot". What are your reactions to these statements? Talk about them with a friend or partner, and keep some kind of record of your thoughts. How will this affect your approach to education at home?

Motivation

 A person will perform any considered action as being preferable to its alternatives.

A sneeze, blink or heartbeat is a reflex action which would take conscious thought to inhibit, if it could be inhibited at all. A soldier incited to charge, a crowd member to riot or the victim of a religious sect to commit suicide is acting by institutionalised adherence, not by personal will. Maybe sending a child to school is part of the same effect. Other actions, however, are considered - the person has a conscious choice and takes it.

There is only one way under high Heaven to get anybody to do anything. And that is by making the other person want to do it.
Dale Carnegie

The action may not be desirable. The schoolboy of ages past who bent over for a caning, the sailor who walked the plank, Socrates who drank hemlock, all did so because they each preferred the perceived results of that action to the perceived results of the alternative.

Generally, of course, we like to think of the most pleasurable option, to the extent that our six-year-old daughter who, given 25p, could spend over an hour in deciding which sweet to buy.

Think back to your own school days (assuming that you did attend school). However diligent you were, can you honestly say there was not a time when a fossil of a teacher was droning on and your attention slipped to what was happening outside the building? Good weather and the chance of an enjoyable game probably detracted from your motivation to attend to a learned discourse on the Peasants' Revolt.

Yet there were probably times when you did not want a lesson to end. Simple fascination for the subject was enough to keep you riveted. Of course you were obliged by the school system to attend and learn, but it will be self-evident that in the latter case more effective learning will occur.

As an example of this, Mary Ann mastered music sufficiently well to pass Grade 5 Piano examinations when she was fourteen. Some thirty years later, she remembers attending piano lessons with dread: the teacher who sat waiting with a wooden ruler to rap her knuckles when her hands dropped out of position, and the threat of being shut in a room every day for an hour to practice. She is no longer able to read music - she can work it out if needed, but in no way can that be called sight-reading. When given written music and asked to play it her reaction is to take flight!

Action! **What did you learn, which you cannot now remember? Did you enjoy the subject at the time? Are there any links between your own enjoyment of a subject and the effectiveness of your learning? If enjoyment and interest are prerequisites to efficient learning, how then do schools achieve this?**

Sometimes schoolchildren will admit to enjoying a particular subject at school, especially if they enjoy the company of the teacher.

Personal enthusiasm for a subject rubs off onto the students, and sometimes this provides the motivating force for learning. Schoolchildren, however, often have an attitude of resignation - we have to be here all day, we have to do this stuff, we can only make the best of it.

A bad day at home is better than a good day in school...
A home-educated child, quoted in *Education Now, News And Review*

Fear Limits Education

Children don't seem to be born fearful... it looks very much as if children catch most of their fears from their elders.

John Holt, How Children Learn

John Holt was writing here from his observations of Lisa, a little girl about 18 months old. He goes on to describe how Lisa was not afraid of bugs - in fact insects held such a fascination for her that she often picked them up to have a closer look! A friend of Lisa's older sister, a girl of about twelve, came to visit. On seeing a spider in the corner of the room, the girl

... began to scream hysterically, and kept on until they got her out of the room and killed the spider. Since then, Lisa has been afraid of all bugs - flies, moths, worms, anything. She has learned her lesson. She doesn't scream or carry on, only draws away from them and doesn't want to have anything to do with them. A part of her curiosity about the world and her trust in it has been shut off. Who can tell when it will turn on again?

John Holt, How Children Learn

Action! Analyse your own fears. How would you react if, say, you and your home-educated child came across a snake or a harmless slow-worm when out for a walk? Would you recoil in horror, and run the risk of stifling a budding zoologist's curiosity? Or would you have the courage to take a closer look at the creature or even pick it up, secure in the knowledge that it can do you no harm? Are you prepared to have a toad in your bathtub while your children observe how he walks, swims, hops, the colour and texture of his skin, shape of his feet, size of his eyes, etc.? As a home educator, no opportunity for learning can afford to be missed.

Confront your own fears before making the final decision to home-educate. They and your ability to overcome them will shape your success or failure as a home educator.

Fear Of Schooling

Another interesting point can be drawn from John Holt's observation of Lisa. Since the experience of seeing the older girl screaming at the unfortunate spider, Lisa keeps away from insects and all crawling things. She "...doesn't want to have anything to do with them."

Spiders - by three-year-old Kester

A parallel can be drawn here between Lisa's behaviour and that of children who, having had a bad experience of school, do not appear to want to do anything when they are at home. Is this the clue to the success/failure of home education at the onset? New home educators, as we have seen, are often under some pressure from LEAs to replicate school at home, as the only way to deliver an effective education. Anxious parents, remembering their own experience of education as a classroom thirty years earlier, find a suitable outfit, stop off at WH Smiths for all the workbooks (preferably with National Curriculum Key Stage Whatever printed boldly on the front) they can lay their hands on, and hurry home thinking *"that should do it"*. At home, little Johnny is reclining on the sofa watching daytime television. Mum appears in her new teacher's attire, spreads the lovely new workbooks on the table and calls Johnny to choose what he would like to do. (Mum has read something somewhere about autonomous education.) Predictably, Johnny doesn't want to know!

Fear of anyone who acts like, sounds like or even looks like a teacher is very real for many children who have just come out of school. That is what they have been taught, quite deliberately, by the system. Teachers depend upon children being fearful, to a certain extent. It is called authority. Without it the whole fabric of the school society would crumble. Trying to home-educate by copying school is likely to fail with children who are afraid. In fact, it may so horrify them that Mum or Dad has turned into one of these monster-teachers but even worse, that the poor child begs to go back to school within a few weeks. Then the parent will become loveable again .

We recently were involved in a situation where a thirteen-year-old boy had been removed from a comprehensive school. His mother related the story: *"James is severely dyslexic, but no one had realised this until he was about eight years old. By then he disliked school so much it was too late - whatever the teachers did, he didn't really want to know about reading and writing."* One afternoon the boy came home from school, threw himself on his bed and sobbed uncontrollably for over an hour. Nothing could console him. When the boy calmed down he told his mother, "It's all the blank pieces of paper. I'm really frightened." This tragic case was of a child whose fear of making a mark on paper was compounded by the school system. Every hour he would go to a different class to be confronted with another blank piece of paper. He could hardly be expected to thrive at home if his well-meaning parents provided plenty of books, paper and pens. Another way of learning has to be applied. There is another way!

Fear And Social Interaction

Fear can also account for much irrational and anti-social human behaviour, such as bullying, racism and sexism. These are not confined to the school playground, but can be found in all walks of adult life as well.

Young children do not seem to notice differences in skin colour or race. A story was once told to us of a father looking at a school photograph with his son. On being asked which of the many scrubbed schoolchildren was the boy's best friend, the descriptions included such aspects as short hair, spectacles, no jumper. He did not include the fact that the friend had the only black face in the picture; that had not been perceived to be a differentiating characteristic.

In our own experience, although we live in a predominantly white area of rural England, a black or brown face will attract less attention from our children than would a person in a wheelchair. Perhaps this is because children are accustomed to looking up to see the faces of adults, or maybe it is the mechanics of the wheelchair which hold more fascination for our children than the disability of its occupant.

At home the onus is entirely upon the parents and close family to convey social and moral values to their children. Whether at home or at school, the family has the greatest influence over the moral development of the child, although when children are schooled there is often a temptation to 'run with the herd' to avoid or minimise the more subtle forms of bullying.

> *One of the most important social skills is the ability to form your own opinions and set of beliefs. If you force your own beliefs and opinions on a child, you are stunting his or her progress. A balance has somehow to be achieved between encouraging this development of personal values and letting your child see that you yourself are able to form moral judgements and personal beliefs.*
> **From the guidelines for home educators, East Sussex, as quoted by Steve Lowden**

The implication here is that home education can be so powerful a tool in indoctrination of children with the opinions and beliefs of the family that it will have the effect of 'stunting their progress'. Why the LEA quoted should feel the need to make such a value-laden statement can only by guessed at. It is certainly not the place of the LEA to do so. It does raise an issue which we all, doubtless, face when we first become parents - the question of our own moral stance and attitudes towards racism, sexism, ageism, etc., and what messages our own behaviour will send to our children.

The National Curriculum provides schools with a structured prescription for the delivery of the Government's brand of education, and it extends to more than the 3 R's. Children are expected to learn social and personal skills, and have knowledge of different cultures and religions. This social aspect of education which is delivered by schools extends to more than the social interaction of the classroom, playing field or playground. Social studies are taught as part of the curriculum in many schools. In taking the decision to home-educate parents need to reassess their values in these areas, and perhaps look again at the quality of education which they are giving through their own behaviour.

Action! Take a critical look at your own values, and decide how you will pass them on to your own children, through coercion ("Do as I say, not as I do!") or by example. Which method of teaching would you consider more effective?

Teachers need to learn a behaviour code quickly. There are things which they might say or do within the company of their friends or in social situations which should never be repeated in school. Whatever their own opinions or beliefs, prejudices or fears, they must appear to be completely unbiased in every respect when at school. The must also watch their language. A confusion arises here when children are actively encouraged to use bad language in 'creative expressive' written work, but might well be suspended from school for using the same words to tell the headmaster (creatively and expressively) what they think of the school.

Even remarks which adults can take in fun or jokes which adults realise are funny because the attitudes they convey are ludicrous may be misconstrued by children. The walls of home educators' homes have ears, 24 hours a day.

> **Action!** Examine your own values alongside developing your own philosophy of education. Can you embark upon home education without making some changes to your own behaviour or adjusting some of your own values?

"You've got to be taught to hate and fear
You've got to be taught from year to year
It's got to be drummed into your dear little ear.
You've got to be carefully taught.

You've got to be taught to be afraid
Of those people whose eyes are oddly made
and people whose skin is a different shade
You've got to be carefully taught.

You've got to be taught before it's too late
before you are six or seven or eight
To hate all the people your relatives hate
You've got to be carefully taught."

O. Hammerstein II, South Pacific

Teacher And Learner

Often, the thought of home education conjures up a nightmare-like scenario in the minds of parents - the long summer holiday which never ends, kids under the feet all day, bored children stuck in front of the television or roaming aimlessly about the house. The alternative view is of the dining room turned into a classroom, the family scrubbed and brushed, sitting up at the table with pencils at the ready, Mother in floral frock and mortar board, chalk in hand, in front of a toy chalkboard.

The latter view is probably the one most frequently pushed upon us by the press. Home educators are too often portrayed as pushy parents, and the children as gifted prodigies who are likely to embark on careers at Oxbridge at the age of eight. It is a complaint often voiced by home-educating families that when the press give coverage to home education, the photographs they want are of the description above - a school at home. The terminology frequently used by many people when talking about education is applicable only to schools. Naturally, as the educational experiences which most of us immediately relate to happened in school, we tend to carry school terminology over into the realm of home education. For example, *"Their Mum teaches them at home"*, or *"You teach them yourself, do you?"* are phrases which we often hear.

'Home-schooling' is another phrase often favoured by those in America - this also gives the impression of school-at-home. Perhaps it stems from the service provided by the radio schools system but the term *'home-schooling'* hardly does justice to the rich variety of education which we have witnessed in home-educating families.

No matter what other interesting things the children might be doing, invariably the press photographer wants a few books on the table and the whole family gathered round Mother, who is pointing to something on a page. Home education in reality is seldom like that.

The parent in the role of teacher does not need to assume the countenance of a teacher.

What Is A Teacher?

When considering *teacher* and all the associated implications of the word, personal experiences and memories play a part.

If you are to take the role of teacher upon yourself, whether through starting a course of professional training, taking up a teaching job, or having the role thrust upon one through opting to home-educate, some self analysis and self evaluation is necessary. Only then can the question *Can I do this job?* Be answered. Before you read on, try this exercise for yourself...

Quick! Think of 'teacher'. What do you see?
Weber & Mitchell, That's Funny, You Don't Look Like A Teacher

Action! Quick! Draw a teacher!

Some researchers working in North America asked a group of teachers and children were asked to 'draw a teacher'. What follows are descriptions of the drawings:

I drew my teacher very traditionally with glasses, conservative clothing, in front of a chalkboard, a woman. I don't think I was thinking about myself as a teacher but more what many elementary school teachers looked like. What a stereotype!
Renee, a student teacher

When asked to either imagine or even draw a picture of a teacher, I still come up with the same figure I used to think of when I was younger...it seems like we can't completely rid ourselves of the traditional ways.
Bridget, a student teacher

Action! Compare your drawing with those described above. Now draw what you think that you in the role of a teacher *should* be.

Teachers represent figures of authority. Primary school teachers are predominantly female (Headteachers, on the other hand are usually portrayed as male), wear dowdy clothes and definitely do not have any life whatsoever outside of school. In fact, seeing a teacher outside of school can be quite a disconcerting experience.

Whilst working as a teacher in an infant school, I recall venturing to the local corner shop one lunchtime. As I paid for my purchases, a young pupil in the school and her mother came into the shop. We exchanged pleasantries, and I walked with them back across the road and into school with the child, a matter of some 50 yards. The child hung her coat up on her peg and then approached me with an air of excitement such as young children have when they are about to impart some great 'secret' or let you in on a new 'discovery' which they have made.

"Miss"

"Yes, Emily."

"Miss...." Emily moved from one foot to the other, wringing her hands in excitement. I waited for the revelation.

"Miss, I saw you...IN THE SHOP!"

Mary Ann

For young children, there is a place for everything and everything should be in its place, i.e. Teachers live in schools, Mums and Dads live at home. Any contradiction to this rule is apt to cause confusion. How, then, will a child who is already distressed by the school experience react when Mummy or Daddy takes on the role (and associated trappings) of teacher, and further to that, does not take him/herself off to school to conduct his frightful business, but stays at home and behaves like a teacher towards the child?

You Don't Have To Be A Teacher

... But As A Home Educator You Must Educate Your Child

The popular image of the teacher is one of an all-knowing, all-seeing being, someone who knows, or at least has access to, all the answers which really matter - in school. As we have already seen, in the mind of the child teachers do not exist out of school, so they cannot be expected to know anything about popular music, the latest street culture or craze, or to understand terms such as 'cool' to mean anything but a low temperature.

If we accept that schooling in general terms equates to a production line at the end of which our children are products, and that external examinations are simply the quality-test which must be passed to prove efficiency of the educational system, teachers are little more than the blue-collar workforce.

It is their task to keep everything on line, and to ensure that as far as possible, each product passes the quality control standards at the end of the conveyor belt. Teachers have been trained in the basic requirements of their job, they learn a few tricks which can be applied along the way (this is called experience), but other than that, they have very few answers.

For parents considering home education, this concept is significant. What new home-educating parents do not have, perhaps, is the basic training and experience of working on the school production line, neither do you have the conveyor belt, the heavy machinery of schooling, or the back-up of a large workforce, teaching unions or a negotiated pay-scale. But you do have the raw materials - your children.

Compare the person who sets out to design and build their own motor car from scratch, using the materials available. The bodywork may be of wood rather than metal because wood is available, the car may be solar powered rather than petrol driven, it may look rather different to the mass produced vehicles which roll out of the Ford car plant in their hundreds every day, but it will work as well, if not better, last longer, be more reliable and be individual. The home-made car would be unlikely to have the flawless paintwork of the factory car. As with school assessment, age/stage development and regular testing, the shiny new car is an outward sign of 'success'. The home educator may not have any such measure to show as an example of success or failure in education, unless they want to. Copies of SATs tests and the whole National Curriculum are available to parents from the DfEE and can be used if wished.

To continue the analogy of the car production line, home educators design their own model, drive it, repair and modify it, and it lasts for a lifetime. Factory-built cars are the mass produced product of a professional designer who works to a detailed specification taking into account costing of raw materials, price to the consumer, economy, suitability for purpose, and has a limited life-time. It has to have the latter, or car production would cease. In human terms, how many times have we heard the phrase "I'm on the scrap heap now" when redundancy strikes? How many people, who think they were set up for life twenty-five years ago with a technological qualification, now find in middle age that the industry has changed beyond recognition and their skills and experience count for naught? The school-based component is difficult to modify and expensive to repair.

> *We have got to stop thinking of our students as products. I once did a study of schools as organisations. I said that the perfect model for a school was a factory, the only trouble was that the students were not the workers but the products - raw materials going through various processes, stamped, inspected for quality, with only certified goods going out. What we failed to do was recycle the rejects.*
> **Charles Handy**

Teaching in school is very different from educating your own children at home. As schooling becomes more like an industry, even to the point where industrialists are now to take over the running of schools, the rift between education and schooling widens.

Home education is lifelong learning

Action! List any ways which you can think of that children learn without formal lessons. Try to identify one way in which you have observed your child learning something over the last 48 hours which has not involved them doing formal written work or homework. How effective do you estimate that learning to be, i.e. how long do you think the child will retain the information, and how might he develop it or build upon the knowledge gained? What measures could you take in assisting him in the process of learning?

Punishments And Rewards

Punishments

Until very recently, and within the experience of many of today's parents, corporal punishment was used in schools. We hope that personal recollections do not extend as far as the birchings that were inflicted, leaving schoolboys scarred for life, both physically and emotionally. Horror stories are still related, though:

> *Headmasters are always very ferce and keep thousands of KANES chiz moan drone. With these they hound and persecute all boys...*
>
> *... Go to study. Kane descend whack gosh oo gosh oo gosh ...*
> **Willans & Searle, Down With Skool!**

> *My own memories of the infant class are of sitting in rows of desks where 40+ children were presided over by an elderly, whiskered, grey-haired lady who patrolled the rows of six-year-olds with a tube of Smarties in one hand and a ruler in the other. She peered in turn at everyone's efforts to write, rewarding some with a sweet and delivering a sharp rap over the knuckles to the unfortunate children whose efforts failed to meet with her expectations.*
>
> *I still clearly recall one afternoon when I can have been no more than five years old. A boy in my class would insist on talking to his neighbour throughout the story-time. In exasperation the teacher said, "Peter, if you cannot keep your tongue still I shall cut it off!" The story continued, and Peter carried on whispering to his friend. The teacher slammed shut her book, stood up, crossed the room and fetched an enamel kidney-shaped bowl, as were frequently used in hospitals in those days, a large wad of cotton wool, a bottle of Dettol and a pair of very sharp looking scissors. She put the whole lot on the desk at the front of the room and summoned the unfortunate Peter. "Now, I said I'd cut your tongue off ..." she began. By this time I was quaking with fear, believing that this woman was actually going to do the deed. Another child started to sob. "Shall I?" (No response from Peter.) "SHALL I?" Peter shook his head, miserably. "Well, go and sit in your place, and don't let me hear you again."*
>
> **Mary Ann**

Such anecdotes may raise a smile, albeit a nervous one, but some serious questions are raised here. We can look back and laugh at the teaching profession as we remember it - perhaps some of the pictures painted are familiar - but if this is not what teachers should be, what should they be? How can the values which are stressed by the teaching profession be duplicated in the home? What about 'discipline', 'basic skills', 'respect', 'punishments' and 'rewards'? If not delivered in the familiar, traditional way as by the old teacher, Smarties in one hand, ruler in the other, how are we as parents going to ensure that any work gets done?

As has been discussed, parents who home-educate do not have to assume the role of teacher. Indeed, in our opinion it would be a serious mistake to do so. Parents should forever remain loving Mums and Dads, interested in the interests and skills of the children, patient, kind and ready to listen and talk to their family rather than teach at them. Certainly, resorting to instilling fear to this level in children is not conducive to a positive love of learning.

Punishment, of course, does not have to be of a physical nature. The withholding of privileges, sweets, pocket money or television can have a greater effect. Often, just to let the child know you are displeased is sufficient. Whatever form the chastisement takes, however, never let it occlude your love for the child.

It is essential to consider the point of the punishment. What right has anyone to punish another individual for not being interested in something?

MUST I be interested in the subject on which I am writing, *or else*? I don't think so. Even if the Big Stick is wielded, is it likely that I would develop an interest? NO!

Punishments for not completing study on time or to standard may not be appropriate for home educators. That is not to imply that there is not a place for discipline in learning, and that is a very different thing. Discipline is control whether it comes from the self or is imposed from a higher authority. Discipline requires patience, self control and self motivation; it has to do with effective management of time and resources for learning, the ability to stick at a tedious task because it is part of a greater, more interesting whole. Discipline comes with age and maturity, and is learnt through following the good examples of patient, organised mentors.

The headmaster at my own junior school had a thing that was rather inaccurately named 'tickling stick'. I think this was a reference to the comedian Ken Dodd, who was very popular then and who carried a feather duster also (and more accurately) called a 'tickling stick'. But the similarity was in name only - the headmaster's was made of leather rather than feathers. Both had a wooden handle, but the headmaster's had three leather thongs and Ken's had none. And the other big difference was that the headmaster didn't say: "Ooh-er, Missus!" as he belted you with it, as Ken is known to do.

What the headmaster did say, rather strangely was, "This is going to hurt me more than it hurts you."

Really! That's what teachers used to say before they hit you. I makes you wonder how they ever became teachers, doesn't it?"

Peter Corey, Coping With School

> **Action!** What do you punish your child for? How do you punish him? How effective is punishment? If the behaviour of your child is not affected by the punishments which you impose, why might this be, and what action could you take to remedy this situation?
>
> How should punishment relate to learning and education at home? Are 'lines', 'detentions' or depravation of privilege (do 'this' or I won't allow you to do 'that') effective strategies? Why do schools use them? Can they be applied at home?
>
> What, in learning at home, deserves 'punishment' - poor work? Unfinished tasks? Refusal to co-operate? Consider how you will deal with any of these potential problem areas.

Rewards

Rewards can come in a variety of guises, but by far the most often used reward is praise. Personal praise, a *"Well done, that's lovely!"*, a smile and a hug works wonders with both children and adults. It is a level of reward which can be immediate, sincere and greatly prized by the recipient, it costs nothing, yet is so very rarely used in schools. If your task is to rebuild a child's self esteem, start with giving praise and plenty of it at every appropriate opportunity.

There is a word of warning here - children are not daft. They know when they have done their best and when they have produced something less than that. You need to catch on to that quickly, for lavishing praise upon your child for producing something which is not up to standard will lose you their respect and credibility.

Student teachers often make this mistake. So thrilled are they that they have actually got a class of children to write or draw at their bidding that the outpouring of praise knows no bounds. The young teacher, anxious to appear friendly and to promote a good relationship, smiles, sings praises and distributes gold stars to everyone. She is really saying, *"Thank you! Thank you! I said 'frog' and you all jumped! It works! Thank you...!"*

Meanwhile, the children are thinking, *"This is a push-over! She is in our power. We'll be able to give her hell next time and get away with it!"*. Go in like a lion, in a short time you will be able to put on lamb's clothing.

Presentation Of Written Records

Whether or not answers are correct, good legible presentation of writing costs nothing but time and care. It is important to develop a sense of taking pride in what one produces and to present it well. One day a letter of application for a job or an examination paper will need to be written, and if it is illegible or badly presented it will not be read by a busy prospective employer or examiner. No matter how good the content, poor presentation will put the reader off before they have begun.

With regard to presentation of written work, home educators need never be anything less than honest. If your child presents you with a scruffy, half-hearted piece of writing ask him, "Is this your best effort?" Set your standards from the very beginning and let it be known, if it would not do at school, it will not necessarily do here either. The problem you then have is, what action should be taken?

Any action you take must depend on why your child has presented you with something less than his best effort. Do consider carefully the reason behind the shortcoming:

- If the activity is note-taking, sketching or experimental, it may be that the activity does not demand a painstaking response.

- Your child may be tired or weary of the activity, in which case trying again at a later time may be the answer.

- He may see no point to the activity. Ask yourself if this is a worthwhile exercise. If it is, why does the child not see it that way?

- He may fail to understand what he is trying to achieve.

- Have you asked him to do something which is too hard or too easy?

- Is there something better to do - for example, does the activity demand sitting at a table indoors when the sun is shining outside and your child would rather be out playing?

> **Action!** How will you reward your child for tasks done well? How will you reward your child for work done as part of the household and family? How will you praise your child's efforts to learn?

Me on the slide in my garden

Hope. 8

What Do I Have To Be, Then?

All you need is love

Lennon & McCartney

Love ...and time, and patience. In a loving environment, given understanding and time, children will learn. The single most important thing which home-educating parents can give their child which schools cannot is time - time to listen, talk, play and work together in a one-to-one situation or as a family. It is not the school environment which facilitates learning, the threat of punishment or the authoritarian figure of the teacher but the motivation of the child. As parents, the best we can do is to provide opportunity, encouragement and stimulation and learning will take place.

Needless to say, the main requirement for a home educator is a total commitment to the upbringing of the child. After that, identifying the qualities required brings to mind the list that the psychologist Carl Rogers attributed to a 'psychologically healthy person':-

1. *An openness to all experience*
2. *An ability to live fully in every moment*
3. *The will to follow their own instincts, rather than the will of others*
4. *Freedom in thought and action, e.g. spontaneity, flexibility*
5. *Much creativity*

Summary

Why are you home-educating?

- Has the school failed?

- Is your child failing in school?

- Are you disillusioned with the system?

- Are you following a different philosophy, perhaps from a particular religious or ethical stance?

How can you justify the belief that home education is better for your child than schooling?

How are you going to educate your child without specialist knowledge or resources?

How are you going to administer discipline?

Define your role as *teacher*

What is your ultimate aim of education? What do you believe an education should achieve, where does it begin and end, and what part do you, as a parent, play in the education of you child?

Chapter Five

The Legality of Home Education

The Law is the true embodiment
Of everything that's excellent.
It has no kind of fault or flaw,
And I my Lords, embody the Law.

W.S. Gilbert, Iolanthe

The Law

In England and Wales the law states that:-

The parent of every child of compulsory school age shall cause him to receive efficient full-time education suitable -

a) to his age, ability and aptitude, and

b) to any special educational needs he may have,

either by regular attendance at school or otherwise.
Section 7, Education Act 1996

Section 7 of the Education Act 1996 is the only legal provision made regarding home education. From this it is clear that the responsibility for ensuring that children receive an education in accordance with the law rests with the parents.

Further to this, it was as long ago as 10th December 1948 that the General Assembly of the United Nations adopted and proclaimed the Universal Declaration of Human Rights, which states:-

Article 26

(1) Everyone has the right to education. Education shall be free, at least in the elementary and fundamental stages. Elementary education shall be compulsory. Technical and professional education shall be made generally available and higher education shall be equally accessible to all on the basis of merit.

(2) Education shall be directed to the full development of the human personality and to the strengthening of respect for human rights and fundamental freedoms. It shall promote understanding, tolerance and friendship among all nations, racial and religious groups, and shall further the activities of the United Nations for the maintenance of peace.

(3) Parents have a prior right to choose the kind of education that shall be given to their children.

This quotation is taken from an international treaty which is not legally enforceable at law. However, point (3) has some relevance to the rights of families to opt for a form of education other than that offered by the school system.

Article 2 of the First Protocol to the European Convention on Human Rights is enacted into English law by the Human Rights Act 1998. It is, however, limited by the reservation which was made by the British government in 1952, and which is also enacted by the Human Rights Act 1998.

Article 2 RIGHT TO EDUCATION

No person shall be denied the right to education. In the exercise of any functions which it assumes in relation to education and to teaching, the State shall respect the right of parents to ensure such education and teaching in conformity with their own religious and philosophical convictions.

PART II RESERVATION

At the time of signing the present (First) Protocol, I declare that, in view of certain provisions of the Education Acts in the United Kingdom, the principal affirmed in the second sentence of Article 2 is accepted by the United Kingdom only so far as it is compatible with the provision of efficient instruction and training, and the avoidance of unreasonable public expenditure.

Dated 20 March 1952

**Made by the United Kingdom Permanent
Representative to the Council of Europe**

These statements give weight to the rights of parents to educate their own children as they wish. It is clear from these documents that home education is legal; in fact, it is the right of any parent to choose to educate his own child at home if he so wishes. The rights of parents to make this choice are not affected by the size and type of home they live in, income, academic qualifications, marital status or relationship with partners, religious faith or following, race or creed. Successful home educators are people of different ages, shapes, sizes, colours and with different jobs and incomes. Home educators can be found living in high-rise flats, narrow boats, caravans, suburban semis, farms, country houses, horse-drawn wagons, palaces which are open to the public - all kinds of homes! The common factor is that they are all parents, and they all educate their own children in their own homes. Unless they are failing to provide an education, they are all within their rights to do so, and to continue doing so for as long as they wish.

There are cases where social services have a right to intervene, such as where a child is being

> *Parents are assumed, in Law, to be competent to teach their children until proved otherwise.*
> **Dr. Steve Lowden, 1995**

Parent is a term widely defined in Section 576 Education Act 1996 and includes those with parental responsibility or those who care for a child. There is no reason in law why anyone who has parental responsibility should not home-educate a child, including those who have adopted children or have care of them. It is not the place of this book to define parental responsibility further, but it is a concept started in the Children Act 1989, and for further definitions we suggest reference to that Act.

Compulsory School Age has been changed since the Education Act 1996; an amendment to the section, s8(2) was made in s52(2)Education Act 1997, which gave the Secretary of State the power to prescribe dates in the year on which children will begin to be of compulsory school age. This he did in 1998, and fixed 31st August, 31st December and 31st March. A child begins to be of compulsory school age if he attains the age of five on one of the prescribed dates or on the next prescribed date following his fifth birthday.

By virtue of s433, schools are not obliged to admit a child as soon as he reaches compulsory school age but may wait until the beginning of the next school term. In such circumstances s433 makes it clear that parents do not breach s7.

In practice, children often begin school in the term in which their fifth birthday falls. In some areas schools take children into the reception class in the year in which they will be five. Thus, it is not uncommon for a child whose birthday is in August to be attending school from a few days after his fourth birthday, although this may not necessarily by full-time attendance and it would not be compulsory.

The school leaving age is governed by the Education Act 1996 and a statutory instrument as follows:

A person ceases to be of compulsory school age at the end of the day which is the school leaving date for any calendar year

(a) if he attains the age of 16 after that day, or

(b) if he attains that age on that day, or

(c) (unless paragraph (a) applies) if that day is the school leaving date next following his attaining that age.

Section 8(3)Education Act 1996

The Secretary of State made an order in 1997 by a Statutory Instrument which provides that *"The school leaving date...shall be the last Friday in June".*

Full-time education does not have a legal definition.. The reference point seems to be the amount of time which children spend in school: 25 hours a week, 38 weeks a year. Some LEAs who give this figure in their guidelines for home-educating families include time spent on homework as well. Using this formula in relation to home education is misleading, as it serves to reinforce the 'school at home is the only way to home-educate effectively' dictum. It also implies that every moment of school is taken up with learning. This is simply not true. To compare the quality of and time spent on effective learning which takes place at home with that of school is at least unfair, if not impossible. How much one-to-one teaching time does each child in school receive? How much contact teaching time do they have? What proportion of school time is spent in taking registers, moving from one classroom to another, getting changed for sports, waiting while various distractions and disruptions are sorted out, books and materials are distributed or any other delay takes place? Whatever the answers to these questions, it is not true to say that every moment is spent in school is filled with an educational activity.

In cases that where home tuition is arranged by the county a maximum of five hours per week of teaching time is considered sufficient. For home educators, education is a continuous, seamless process. It starts as soon as the children are awake, and contact teaching time ends when the children go to sleep. Home educators do not have holidays, dinner breaks, playtimes or training days. On balance, it is unlikely that a home-educating family who takes its responsibilities seriously will be actively involved in education for a shorter time than children who attend school.

Summary Of The Law

1. All parents have the right to choose the kind of education they desire for their own child, including education other than at school. Parents may educate their own children wherever they wish.

2. Children of compulsory 'school' age as defined by the law have a right to education under the terms of the law. To deny a child that right is in breach of the law. Education does not necessarily have to take place in school.

Registration and Deregistration

If a child is not registered in school, parents are under no legal obligation to inform the Local Education Authority (LEA) of their intention to home educate. For example, if the parents of a four year old child do not wish the child to attend school for whatever reason, they do not need to inform either a school or the LEA of their decision. They are entitled to keep the child at home with them for as long as they wish to do so and continue educating him as they wish indefinitely.

When a child has been registered at school, however, formal deregistration clears the way for parents who wish to home-educate. This is as simple yet formal procedure, and must be carried out if the child is no longer to attend the school. If a child misses even a day at school before being formally deregistered parents are liable to prosecution for failing to ensure that they send their child to school regularly contrary to s444 Education Act 1996 (the ordinary truanting provision). If they are prosecuted it is not a defence to say that they have been home educating.

To deregister a child from school in England and Wales a formal letter addressed to the 'proprietor' of the school is needed, explaining that as from (date) the child will be educated at home. No reason for the decision need be given. Upon receipt of such a letter the parent's duty to ensure that their child attends school regularly is over.

2 Acacia Gardens,
Nowhere Really,
Somewhere Else,
30th February

Dear Sir,

I write to inform you of my decision to take responsibility for my son Fred's continuing education myself, as is my right under s7 Education Act 1996. As from 31st February, 2000, Fred will be educated at home.

Please confirm receipt of this letter and that in accordance with regulation 9(1)(c) Education (Pupil Registration) Regulations 1995, you have removed Fred's name from the school register.

A copy of this letter has been forwarded to the Chairman of the Governors.

Yours faithfully,

W Shakespeare.

Figure 1: Sample Letter of Deregistration

The letter is an important official document and should be treated as such. We recommend that a copy be kept, and proof of delivery to the proprietor of the school be obtained, either by sending the letter by recorded delivery or by delivering it into the hands of the proprietor, noting the date and time of delivery, and obtaining a confirmation of receipt from him.

You may wish to use this opportunity to thank the school for their efforts with your child to date. This is also an opportunity to put in a formal request for the child's school workbooks, test results or personal belongings.

Many parents have experienced a sudden and severe change in attitude from schools once they have let it be known that they intend to home-educate. They report instances where previously friendly members of staff have 'cut them dead' when they have called to collect their children's belongings, and workbooks have mysteriously vanished. This leaves parents completely bereft of any clue as to the standard of work which their children are capable of, or the level at which they might pitch further study. The moral is perhaps, to find an opportunity to inspect workbooks and remove personal possessions prior to deregistration, rather than attempting to reclaim things afterwards. These claims may have some bearing on the wisdom of telling the school of your possible intentions before formally deregistering a child.

When the school receives a letter such as the one above a child will be effectively deregistered and parents can expect that the LEA will be informed. If your home address is not in the same administrative area as the school - for example, if the school is in one county and your home is in another - your LEA may not necessarily know of your choice to home-educate. Similarly, if you deregister your child, move away and then choose to home-educate, you are under no obligation to inform the LEA in your new home area of your decision. Should you move to the UK from overseas you are likewise under no obligation to inform the authorities.

It is not hard to appreciate the difficulty which researchers and other interested parties have in determining a reliable number of children who are home-educated at any one time. While so many families remain unknown to the LEAs, and many join more than one support group, join for a short period only or do not choose to join a support group at all, no figures of home educators are available. Unless registration is made compulsory for home educators, this is likely to remain the case.

It is at the point of receipt of the letter requesting deregistration that there appears to be some discrepancy between what is stated in the Education Act and what happens in practice.

Case Law (Phillips v Brown, Divisional Court (20th June 1980, unreported), Judicial review by Lord Justice Donaldson... established that an LEA may make informal enquiries of parents. One might imagine that this *'informal enquiry'* would take the form of a letter or telephone call requesting information.

> *Of course, such a request is not the same as a notice under s37(1) of the Education Act 1944 (now s437 (1) of the 1996 Education act) and parents will be under no duty to comply. However, it would be sensible for them to do so.*
> **Lord Donaldson**

In fact, this *'informal request'* is seldom, if ever, put into practice by the LEAs, and new home educators may expect to receive requests for detailed plans, timetables, and schemes of work which relate to the kind of regime operating in schools. These are often accompanied by misleading and sometimes incorrect 'guidelines' which are issued to home educators by LEAs.

What Happens After Deregistration?

When the letter requesting deregistration of a child is received by the proprietor of a school, the child no longer need attend the school, and the school has ten working days in which to inform the LEA of the deregistration of the pupil (reg. 13 (3)).

The LEA usually makes contact with the parents of the child within the next half-term of school time. Normally, this is the initial *'informal enquiry'* (although as we have already stated, it seldom appears very informal), but sometimes parents will have an unannounced visit from an Education Welfare Officer (EWO). If an EWO turns up on the doorstep home educators have no reason to furnish him with any further information than to confirm the names of the children who are being home-educated at that address. Home educators may expect the LEA to communicate in writing with the parents of recently deregistered children resident within the administrative area. Some LEAs communicate with each other, so if your home is not in the same area as the school from which your child has been deregistered, it still may be that you will be contacted by your local LEA. In any case, provision is made in the law for LEAs to make *'informal enquiries'* and when they do parents are bound to respond. Details and evidence of the education offered at home must be given if requested.

The kind of information which home educators present to the LEA is up to them; the LEA may not choose what evidence of education it will or will not accept. The only task of the LEA is to see that the evidence offered satisfies them that a suitable education is being offered by the parents under the terms of s7; not that it is being implanted into the child. For example, s7 applies to all parents, and yet no one prosecutes the parents of children who fail to absorb the teaching they get in school. In this respect, it could be argued that there is no need to involve the children at all, as the LEA should be able to glean all the information required from the response of the parents to their informal enquiry.

Certainly, the LEA has no grounds for demanding to visit the home of a home-educating family. Neither can it ask to see written evidence of children's learning, to assess or test the home-educated children in any way, or to witness 'lessons'. The onus here is not upon the LEA to provide evidence that parents are failing in their duty to give an education under s7; it is for the parents to show that the requirements are being met..

Neither does the LEA have any powers to 'pass' or 'fail' a home-educating family. Should it be dissatisfied with the evidence presented the LEA may make a formal request for the parents to demonstrate that they are providing a suitable education. If, after that, the LEA is still not satisfied, it can issue a School Attendance Order (SAO) which requires the parent to register the child at a nominated school. If this is ignored the LEA may then prosecute the parents, in which case they would be required to present evidence of provision of education to the court. If the court, on the balance of probabilities, finds the educational provision at home lacking, a fine may be imposed, and ultimately a child may be forced to return to school if a care order or educational supervision order is imposed.

Ultimately, the LEA cannot prevent any family from home-educating; only a court can do that. Neither is there any provision for the LEA to assess or monitor the education which the parents offer.

The duties of the LEA are defined in the wording of s437 Education Act 1996, i.e. it is the duty of the LEA to issue a SAO if…

> *…it appears to the LEA that the parents are not providing a suitable education, and when asked to supply evidence the parent refuses to do so.*

A further duty is imposed upon LEAs as a result of the enactment of the School Standards and Framework Act of 1998, Section 5 of which inserts into the EA1996 a new section, 13A, which gives the LEA a duty to promote high standards in primary and secondary education, and requires the LEA to exercise its function relating to the provision of education for children of compulsory school age, whether they are being educated at school or otherwise. It therefore includes home educators *"with a view to promoting high standards"*.

To summarise:

1. The LEA may make informal enquiries as to the educational provision which parents of home-educated children intend to give.

2. If it is dissatisfied with the response provided, a formal request may be made, a School Attendance Order may be issued and, if prosecution of the parents follows, it will be for the court to decide on the balance of probabilities, whether or not the parents are fulfilling their duties under s7.

3. Only the court can prevent parents from home-educating, and children can only be forced to attend school by the issuing of a Care or Educational Supervision Order from the courts.

4. Nowhere in the wording of the EA1996 is there any reference to the LEA having any duty to 'monitor' or to 'assess' the educational provision of parents who are home-educating. Having satisfied itself that the educational provision offered is sound, that should be the end of the matter, unless something is brought to its attention that indicates that circumstances have changed since it was last satisfied with the provision being made. It is arguable that the LEA has no ongoing duty to monitor.

Scotland

In Scotland the procedure is rather different. Parents who wish to deregister a child from a public (state) school should write first to their local Director of Education, stating that they intend to educate their child at home as is their right under s.30 of the Education (Scotland) Act 1980, and asking for removal of the child's name from the school register as soon as possible. A copy of the letter may be sent to the head of the school to make him aware of your intentions, and you may wish to outline the educational provision which you intend to make. This is the time to mention any support which you have sought, e.g. from groups like Schoolhouse, the home education support group specifically for Scotland (see Resources at the end of this book).

Would-be home educators in Scotland need the permission of the Education Committee before a child can be deregistered from a public school, and the authorities will need to satisfy themselves that you are both serious in your intention to home-educate and able to provide an efficient full-time education for your child before permission is granted. Having written to the Director of Education the education authority may send you a copy of its guidelines (see LEAs Behaving Badly, page 85) and asked to co-operate with the authority in agreeing to a home visit, during which they will wish to discuss your decision and commitment to home education. Following this, a report will be presented to the Education Committee or local council, recommending or refusing that consent be granted.

The Scottish Executive has declined to provide any guidelines to the local authorities as, they say, interpretation of the law is a matter for the courts. As there has never been a court case in Scotland, and it seems unlikely that the landmark English case (Harrison v. Stevenson, Worcester 1981) would be taken into account in Scotland, the interpretation of the law in Scotland falls upon the individual councils. The ease with which home education may be established within Scotland is, then, something of a lottery at the moment, dependent upon the interpretation which your local council put upon the law.

A difficulty with needing the permission of the local authority occurs when a child is suffering extreme stress due to school, or school phobia. Parents have a legal obligation to ensure that a child attends school until his name has been removed from the register, unless a *reasonable excuse* can be shown. If a child is sick, or if his health is suffering through school attendance it should be possible for a medical certificate to be issued from the GP, and that would constitute a 'reasonable excuse' to keep the child at home. Should this be the case, our advice is to keep records of anything which is being done to educate the child at home, pending deregistration.

Special Educational Needs (SEN)

When a child is registered at a special school, parents must inform the LEA of any intention to home-educate. In these cases the LEA have to give their consent (Regulation 9(2) Education (Pupil Registration Regulations, 1995 ([S. 1995/2089]) only when referring to children with SEN do the LEA have responsibility for their education and then only if it maintains a statement. The purpose behind this is ultimately to protect the interests of the children, allowing the LEAs to satisfy themselves that the special educational needs of the child will continue to be met when school attendance has ceased. As with deregistration from mainstream school, parents are entitled to reasonable time and opportunity to show that suitable education can be provided at home. They should be given sufficient information to enable them to meet the demands of the LEA relating to their provision.

Children with statements may need the statement reassessed and the wording changed slightly when they begin home education. Statements need to be reviewed annually, and it may be that, once out of school, there is no longer any need for a statement and it can be terminated, by application to the LEA. Should an LEA refuse to give their consent an appeal may be made by the parent to the Secretary of State.

The Involvement Of The LEA

An LEA Home Education Manager has an unenviable job. There are no clear guidelines given to LEAs on this matter from the DfEE, and no general agreement amongst LEAs on the amount of involvement which they have with home education. The manager must be satisfied that an education is being received by the registered children within the authority yet cannot demand to see written work, test, assess or hear a child read.

Without the co-operation of the parents the monitoring role of the LEA is well-nigh impossible.
Richard Bates, 'Education Otherwise: The LEA's Role In Home Education' - National Foundation For Educational Research, February 1996.

There should be no need for home educators to feel threatened by the LEA. Remember that any observations they may make are their only their opinion, and you do not have to take any advice offered. Having said that, they are professional educators and may have some constructive comments to make.

To summarise, the extent of the involvement which your LEA will expect to have with your home education will depend upon where you live. In this respect, it is something of a lottery at the present time. Some LEAs are working towards developing a very good relationship with home educators, offering practical advice and even providing of 'drop-in' centres, liaising with the Library service and negotiating flexi-time in schools. Others have a far more draconian attitude towards home educators, and seem intent upon returning home-educated children to school. Some adopt a minimalist policy, discharging their legal duty of monitoring and doing no more.

We took Government advice about the system and opted out, but not in the way intended by the Tories, from LEA control. We went one step further, and have opted out of Government interference in our children's education. The LEA maintains its responsibility by inspecting us regularly, but that is all. What we do, and how we do it, is now basically down to us. During the anxious Spring of 1991 that seemed a heavy burden, but in reality it is not.

It is not a heavy burden because I am confident I know what my children need now. They need challenges, and they need to extend their imaginations: where are these needs addressed in the hierarchical National Curriculum?
Katherine Trafford, 'Starting Out', from 'Learning from Home education.'

LEAs Behaving Badly

So far in this chapter we have examined the rights of Home Educators as set out under the terms of the Law. It should be stressed that the Law relating to Home Education in Scotland is somewhat different, and currently under review, following devolution. However, in our experience of the treatment of home educators in England and Wales, it appears that there are few, if any, LEAs who adhere to the Education Act 1996 as we understand it.

First, we have yet to encounter an education authority which makes 'informal enquiries' of new home educators. This is not to say that there are none; it is simply that the writers have not yet heard of any. In practice, having deregistered a child from school parents might expect to receive a written request for information from the LEA through the post within six weeks. This will probably take the form of a letter on official headed paper, and may request an initial written response, which will be followed by a home visit from an LEA Advisor and/or EWO. Often, the response required involves the parent being asked to complete a school-type timetable, detailing the activities which the child will be doing over a typical five day working week period, using the same time-schedule as that used in schools.

Further information may be requested, regarding books to be used in supporting study, names and qualifications of people involved in the tutoring of the child (including the qualifications of the parents), details of any 'social' provision, opportunities for physical education and sport, music, drama and of course, details of when and how social interaction with the child's peer group will occur.

Sometimes the LEA wish to have details of the size and layout of the homes of home educating families, and request details of where activities such as Art and Science will take place. Is there space for a child to read or work quietly and undisturbed? Are there younger or older siblings, or other people sharing the home, and if so, how will home education take place within the space available?

It is hard to see how such information constitutes an 'informal enquiry', especially when the initial response is expected to take the form of a timetable, and often accompanied by 'guidelines' which give details of the amount of hours school children spend in school, and the merits of the National Curriculum. Some LEAs tell new home educators that they are bound to use the National Curriculum, and work towards GCSE and SATs, and far too often we are contacted by confused and frightened home educators who have been given information by LEAs which is simply incorrect.

Perhaps it is intended that this kind of information given out and requested from parents is to be helpful. In some cases that may be so, but very often the information in the guidelines which are produced by LEAs is at least misleading if not blatantly inaccurate. Arriving on the doorstep of a new home educator and shrouded in all the trappings of officialdom - headed notepaper, quotes from acts, quotes from the National Curriculum, plenty of educational jargon and direct comparison with school - the LEA guidelines look far more like a prescription for home education. Often they include thinly veiled threats about School Attendance Orders, court summonses and fines. It is not uncommon for LEAs to give a time limit for responses to their forms, or to send an Education Welfare Officer (EWO) to call upon families who have only made an enquiry about the possibility of home education. These hardly constitute *'informal enquiries'*, and parents who are new to home education are often left feeling very intimidated by the LEA. In fact, the home educator may have cause to wonder if bullying stops at the school fence or whether it spills over into the LEA.

Paradoxically, the reasons behind the LEA's behaviour towards home educators may stem directly from their perceived duties of monitoring and child care. Underneath this is perhaps another agenda; that of maintaining the status of elective home education as the government's best kept secret, a fitting phrase we heard from a parent enquiring about home education.

In recent years the profile of home education has been raised considerably mostly through the attention of the press. The temptation for parents is to remove children from schools when problems occur, and some (but by no means all) families take on the responsibility for education without having thought it through properly, talked with or read anything by other home educators, and with no clear idea as to an educational philosophy or strategy.

It is this 'home education in anger' which the LEAs appear to be attempting to guard against in their initial approach to families. We have some sympathy with the concerns of the LEAs on this matter, although we remain unconvinced that suggesting the use of a school timetable is either appropriate or an effective way forward. Here we see the concept of 'only one way' manifesting itself again.

Providing a timetable forces parents to focus in on precisely what they are going to be doing.
LEA Home Ed manager.

If education depended upon timetables and curricula then this would be acceptable, but children learn in many different ways. Implied imposition of a school timetable may be counterproductive to children who have been damaged in some way by schooling. Similarly, pressure to become a teacher overnight, fully conversant in educational jargon and philosophy, is unlikely to boost the confidence of many parents.

Efficient full-time education is not dependant upon the provision of a 'school at home' situation, as we shall discuss later in this book.

Neither in Scotland, nor England and Wales are parents under any obligation to:

- give reasons for wishing to home-educate,

- provide evidence of formal qualifications,

- follow any imposed curriculum or timetable,

- make provision for children to take external examinations,

- test or assess children or provide evidence of progress,

- agree to a home visit from the authorities.

Parents may be asked to provide the local authorities with some form of evidence that effective full-time education is taking place at home. Evidence does not have to be in the form of written work: exercise books, folders of school-type work and work books. It could be presented as an audio or video tape, photographs, drawings and paintings, or a scrapbook. Dates on work are important. Keeping such a record is essential in case any legal dispute should arise.

...there is a tendency for the LEA to project what it knows best, the school morphology and framework, into the home - the concept that a child educated otherwise will be working in a miniature school with all its trappings.
Steve Lowden

It is the great triumph of compulsory government monopoly mass-schooling that....only a small number can imagine a different way to do things.
John Taylor Gatto

Contacting The LEA

As has already been shown, the responsibility for contacting the LEA in the first instance lies with the school. But there may be occasions when a the LEA does need to be contacted, for information about the procedures and provision in a specific area, to make or change appointments or for more general enquiries. Unless you know the name of the Home Education Manager responsible for your area, getting in touch with the right person can be very difficult. Start with the telephone directory - a letter addressed to the Home Education Manager is unlikely to reach the person who you wish to contact, so establishing a NAME is important. Some LEAs are listed under the *'Education'* section in the County or Borough council pages of the telephone directory. If *'Education'* is not listed, try the line for General Enquiries. Ask to speak to the person who monitors children who are educated at home. This will usually confuse the receptionist, so be prepared to clarify your request by putting it in several different ways - you might try such terms as 'education otherwise', 'education out of school', 'home education' or 'children whose parents teach them at home'. Be patient, and be prepared to spend some time on the 'phone while you are put through to various departments.

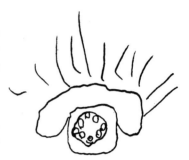

No standard term is used by LEAs to define home education. It might be referred to as:

- Education Other Than At School (EOTAS)

- Education Out Of School (EOOS)

- Education Otherwise (EO)

- Home and Hospital Education

It can be a demoralising experience for a new home educator to find that first, the department which deals with your problem is unknown to the switchboard at the council, and second, you are being put through to all sorts of other inappropriate people:-

"You want accounts..."

"Oh, you mean exclusions and admissions"

"Behavioural support...just a moment, I'll put you through..."

"I'll try psychologists for you, caller..."

"Hullo, Pregnant Schoolgirls...!"

When you do get through, start by checking that you are speaking to an advisor who does the home visits, rather than an Education Welfare Officer, and get the name of the person responsible, thus avoiding a similar pantomime should you seek future contact.

Many LEAs have no budget for the overseeing of home education, and no resources to offer to home educators. The human resources and time devoted to home education are minimal - Home Education Managers may allow at the most one or two days a week to carrying out their task, most have less than that. With the current number of known home educators this provision is clearly inadequate, yet the number of home educators is growing steadily.

Few LEA Managers who have responsibility for home education have had any training at all for their job, and few have any prior knowledge of home education option, what it means in terms of provision or the Law, and what alternative learning strategies might be adopted by home educators.

Many, but not all, home education managers are qualified teachers Their experience of education differs - some have only ever taught in secondary or further education and may have little concept of early years learning. Few are fully aware of the opportunities for learning which have come about recently through the widening availability of Information Technology, and most, although wishing to appear open-minded about the issue of learning, still base their assessments upon the role model of the school, with which they are most familiar.

> *LEAs do not always appreciate that alternative approaches to educating children....may nevertheless be appropriate for some pupils.*
> **Richard Bates**

Further to all this, the law, as we have seen, comes down firmly on the side of the home-educating families. Any successful intimidation on the part of the LEAs depends upon families being ignorant of their rights.

When Initial Enquiries Are Responded To

When the LEA receive a response to their initial enquiries they will contact the family again and arrange a mutually convenient time when a home visit can take place. The LEA have no right of entry to your home, neither can they demand to interview alone, test or formally assess your child. They cannot demand to see any evidence of written work by the child. In practice, it is always a good idea to keep any of the child's work with his name and the date clearly written on it.

Keep records of reading and book lists, number work, or an education diary with notes of the things you have done.

Relating To The LEA

First, become familiar with your rights as a home educator in law. Only when equipped with this information can you decide for yourself how to proceed with your LEA. Do you wish to develop a relationship of mutual respect and trust, or would you rather stick firmly to your rights within the law and run the risk of antagonising the LEA?

Secondly, spend some time on considering your own educational philosophy. Should education mean 'school at home', or do you believe it is something wider than this? What do you feel education ought to achieve, both in the long and short term? If you feel that schooling has failed your child either academically, socially or both, try to identify the precise nature of your grievances with the system, and think of what you could offer your child at home which would at least be equal to school, if not better.

Thirdly, you must decide how to reply to enquiries from the LEA. Here again you have several choices. Upon receipt of a standard letter and forms you could:-

i. Fill everything in as fully as possible and return it within the stated time.

ii. Fill in what you can, e.g. child's name and address, date of birth, ex-school, etc.. Write *Not Applicable* across timetables and requests for details, and provide a covering letter briefly stating your personal philosophy in the light of what you have found out about home education.

iii. Refuse to co-operate with the LEA, stating clearly the law as it stands and offering to provide some evidence of ongoing education at home as soon as reasonably possible.

It is your choice. Having said that, we recommend the second option.

The danger of the first option is that decisions will have to be made prematurely; when you have committed your plan to paper the LEA is liable to hold you to it. The third option, although it is legal, will antagonise the LEA, resulting in a series of stress-inducing letters from them

In the light of our own experience, the middle course provides the most constructive way of satisfying the initial demands of the LEA without committing too many unknowns to paper. It allows you to make it very clear that you know your rights, are receiving support from a home education group, and are working towards developing your own personal educational philosophy. It also paves the way for further positive feedback on both sides in the future.

It is surely infinitely more desirable to work together with your LEA than to be in a situation where you live in fear and suspicion of each other. If at all possible, try to build up a relationship with the LEA representative so that they can get on with their job, and you can get on with educating your child on a daily basis.

Summary

- A child between the ages of 5 and 16 must receive an education suitable to his "age, ability and aptitude" and any Special Educational Needs, *"Full time"* is not defined under the law.

- In England and Wales, most children can be deregistered from school upon receipt by the school of a letter from the parents. The LEA should be informed by the school.

- The LEA is entitled to make informal enquiries regarding the educational provision made by the parents for the child. This is usually as a form which parents are asked to complete and return.

- Upon receipt of the completed form, the LEA will request a meeting with the family. This can take place as a home visit, but it does not have to. Parents have the right to request a meeting elsewhere, or they can offer to submit any evidence of education and refuse to meet the LEA at all.

- The LEA have no powers to pass or fail a home-educating family. If they are not satisfied with the provision made, it can issue a School Attendance Order (SAO). In such a case the onus would be upon the parent to convince the court on a balance of probabilities that the child was receiving an education in accordance with the law.

- The LEA may request another visit at a later date. There is no requirement in the law for this to take place.

Chapter Six

Getting Started With Home Education

From quiet homes and first beginning,
Out to the undiscovered ends...

Hilaire Belloc, Dedicatory Ode

Monday Morning

So, you have taken your child out of school. You have started to work out a philosophy, found out about the law, contacted the support groups, and talked to other home-educating families. The decision has been made, the letter has been written, the child has been informed and the celebrations are in full swing.

Somewhere in the back of your mind is the nagging thought which sounds something like, *OK, but what am I going to do on Monday morning?*. You are not alone. Your child is wondering this too, so is your partner, your friends and relatives start to watch you closely, and very soon your bank manager will be wondering what has become of the pay cheque which has failed to adorn your account and why you should have given up a decent job.

The answer to the bank manager is straightforward: *The happiness and well-being of my child comes before my job and income.*

The other questions have answers which are much less clear cut. *What am I going to teach him?* Is a big enough puzzle for you to face without the need for all the conflicting demands, real or imaginary, which you feel are already beginning to bear down upon you from your family, friends, curious neighbours, critical teachers and parents from the school. And then there is the Local Education Authority. They Inspect You, don't they...?

If you have got this far, let us face it, you are probably committed to home education. School does not work out for your child. You have already made some pretty bold decisions. Perhaps you have surprised yourself - you may have never had a radical thought in your head before, or made any move which might be construed as seditious or irresponsible. Now here you are, on the very brink of joining the growing numbers of home educators.

...if you have suddenly decided to withdraw your child from school the prospect can be daunting, especially in the case of older children. According to one parent, "It's suddenly Monday morning and what are you going to do?"
Alan Thomas, Educating Children At Home

You Can Educate Your Own Child

Perhaps you did not do very well at school yourself. Maybe you left formal education as quickly as possible and with very few qualifications. Can you honestly believe that you are capable of educating your own child?

The answer to this is a resounding, "YOU CAN!" Parents educate their children unaided from the moment the child arrives. Think back to the days before your child started school. What did he learn? To speak, to walk, to dress and undress himself, feed himself - well those at least. How did he learn all this? From watching, listening, copying actions and testing responses for himself. Long before your child reached school age you had already taught him one of the most complex things that he will ever learn - language - and you did it without anyone telling you how, but by talking to and listening to your child.

We teach them to walk, talk, feed and dress themselves, all the hard stuff. When that basis is laid we can't be given the credit for teaching them two plus two.
Alan Thomas, Educating Children At Home

Now you have to pass them on to someone else, so start to recognise what you can do and tackle what you cannot do, and your education will extend alongside your child's. That is what home education is all about.

Freedom

Opting to home-educate could be likened to winning the National Lottery - at a stroke all the restrictions of the school curriculum and timetable are removed. What is the child to study, how, and when? All this will become apparent as time passes, you and your child become reacquainted with each other and a working partnership is established. Of course learning must take place, but before that can happen many children and parents need a period of deschooling (See page 103). So on that first 'Monday morning' of home education, it may be that the only effective action which can be taken is to do nothing. Have a holiday! Relax. This is perfectly normal - after all, both your child and yourself have gone through considerable turmoil in coping with school, coming to the decision to home-educate, reading the books, confronting the authorities, writing the letter... You deserve a break. Treat it as such, and set a date when you expect to start work in, say two or three weeks' time.

No period in history has been more child orientated than ours, nor produced parents who regard themselves as so inadequate. After generations when they could do no wrong, many parents now feel themselves incapable of doing anything right.
David Lewis 'How to be a Gifted Parent'

In reality, no one does *nothing*. No matter what you do, there are opportunities to talk and listen to each other, to get to know each other over again, to work together in a co-operative way, to think and reflect. This is how we learn, and these activities should never be underestimated. Involve your child in the running of the house - expect him to look after his own belongings and his own space at least. It is not unreasonable to ask even a young child to make his own bed and tidy his own room, even if he needs some help. Dispensing with school means that you no longer have the 'state baby-sitting service' at your disposal. Unless you make some other child-care arrangements, your child will be with you wherever you go. This can be frustrating if you are in a hurry. Young children cannot be hurried, so leave plenty of time for appointments and even for shopping trips, as they will inevitably take longer.

The day-to-day experiences which you have in running your home may be mundane to you, but they will be new and fascinating to your child. Encourage him to take part and help with the tasks which you need to do. Every activity presents an opportunity for learning.

Use this time of mutual deschooling to begin noticing how your child learns and where his interests and skills are. Keeping a journal or home education diary will help you to do this, and provide some evidence of on-going education for the LEA. Home educators are not required to keep records or to monitor progress in learning, so whether or not you choose to keep any is entirely up to you, although, as we have seen, it can be valuable to do so. The following ideas have been developed in direct response to demands for help from new home educators who do wish to have some reference points and some form of record.

Keep A Home Education Diary Or Journal

Using The Journal

Writing a journal or home education diary may not be as straightforward as you first imagine. It is tempting to overlook perfectly valid learning opportunities which occur in every home every day and dismiss them as insignificant events - just part of everyday life. There will be opportunities for extending the education of yourselves and your child to outside the home environment, perhaps by visits to local museums or places of interest or trips farther afield. These should be noted in the journal, but this kind of activity is unlikely to take place every day. Most days will be taken up with the mundane routine of running the house. That is not to say that there is no potential for learning to take place, and keeping a detailed journal will help you to identify the opportunities which exist and assess how you use those with your child.

We just went out and did lots of things. I kept a journal of all the learning things. At the end of six months I drew up a chart in readiness for the next visit. I was flabbergasted at the amount of learning taking place, for example through discussion, experience, being out and about. The feedback was phenomenal.
Alan Thomas, Educating Children At Home

This should not be a time-consuming exercise. Half an hour each evening set aside for the analysis of what has happened and the writing up of the journal should be plenty, although you may find that it takes longer if you get carried away with enthusiasm for the job!

What To Write And Why

What you write down is up to you but this sample may help you get started. We have divided the sheet into a number of columns:

Date: Comments:

Time	Activity What did we do?	Dialogue What did we talk about?	Learning Opportunities Questions/Answers arising	School Subjects N - Number L - Language Sc - Science G - Geography H - History A - Art M - Music DK - Don't Know	Child Interest Level G - Good OK - Average P - Poor
11:30	Car journey to town (27 miles) with 8 yr old Charlie	Grandfather has had a stroke - Charlie wants to know what has happened. I explain that one side of his body doesn't work any more. Eyes - how they work - brain Lenses - rainbows - spectrum - length of light	-> Does Grampy's eye work? Charlie knew that the eye, as a camera, viewed everything upside down and the brain made sense of the image. Discussed lenses. Charlie used his magnifying glass to see at which point the image turned upside down. Discussed refraction of light. Why things in the distance appear blue/grey. Change in dialogue at 35 mins. Intensity of colour. Reminded Charlie of a song and he sang the rest of the way.	Sc: Biology (strokes, brain, eyes blood supply, oxygen), Physics (lenses, light, spectrum) A: perspective N: distance in inches/miles, related to spatial awareness G: horizon, curvature of the Earth, landscape - identifying hills, escarpment, valley, direction, compass points M: the song which Charlie remembered was - "North, South, East and West, Think of whichever you love the best, Forest, Vale, High <u>Blue</u> Hill"	G

Use the other side of this sheet for any additional comments

Figure 2: Home Education Journal

DATE   You are making a record of what has happened in order to satisfy your own curiosity and to provide evidence to an LEA manager of an ongoing full-time education. You may have neither the time nor the inclination to write down everything which has happened during the course of a day. You do not need to, but a journal giving a record of at least some events of the day will assist you in focusing your thoughts on the value of the activities you share and the conversations you have with your child. It will also show to the LEA that you are making an effort to organise your ideas about home education.

COMMENTS   Write a brief comment about the situation in your home that day, e.g. *All late up this morning, husband left without breakfast in a bad mood*, or *Lovely sunny day, could not face housework, went into garden*. Include a comment about the weather - experienced teachers invariably dread windy days as the wind puts many children into a bad mood for learning. It may even be that the phases of the moon have an effect on your child - if you have noticed regular patterns of difficult behaviour, try to find a link with some external force. Diagnosis of this will help you planning for future activities.

TIME   Make a note of the time of day when an activity took place. After a few days you may find that a pattern emerges of times when your child is most receptive to concentrated effort and times when they are happier to listen quietly. When do they need frequent breaks and when do they prefer to play, or to demand your constant attention? If you can see patterns emerging you will soon realise when there is little point in expecting them to sit and work at any activity, or listen quietly to a story, or when you can expect to have time to yourself.

ACTIVITY   Keep this brief, e.g. *washing up breakfast things, loading the washing machine, making the beds*. Over time it will show that you have both been involved in a variety of activities, unless, of course, every day you write the same thing in this space, in which case perhaps you may need to make some adjustments to your routine! For your own interest and record, consider even taking a photograph of these activities taking place and attaching it to the journal. A disposable camera kept for this purpose is small and cheap, better still is a digital camera which, although expensive to purchase in the first instance is cheap to run and an invaluable home educator's accessory to a home-computer.

DIALOGUE   Keep this note brief, too, but try to record every subject discussed. This is only to jog your own memory and if you would like to make a more detailed record of a specific conversation use the space on the back of the sheet or a separate piece of paper, or try leaving a tape recorder running in a not too obvious place.

Q&A   Jot down the questions which arose from your conversation, and try to identify the subjects which were discussed. The main consideration here is not whether or not you know the answers to the questions your child asks, but how you use his questions to ascertain the level at which he is thinking and capable of understanding, which questions it might be worthwhile following up, and how you are going to find out more information to fill in the gaps in your own knowledge.

SUBJECTS   Draw lines from the previous column to link with the familiar school subjects. You can use abbreviations for these to save time. Try to look for patterns again - how many questions or how much discussion relates to each subject area? Does a simple conversation over a single activity bring up a variety of 'school' subjects and at what level?

INTEREST   This is partly to relate back to the level of the child's receptiveness at any time of the day, and partly to help you to determine the kind of activities, practical, problem solving or purely academic, which interest your own child. Using a code will save time again.

NOTES   You might like to make any other comments about your own performance or any further observations about your child on the other side of the paper. How might you, for instance, do things differently next time? What mistakes did you make in that particular activity - did you expect too much or too little of your child? Was the task given at the right pitch, at the right time, and were you suitably prepared and equipped? As an adult, you are able to embark upon a task and abandon it easily if, for example, you find that you do not have all the materials needed for the job. For a child, however, this can be very disappointing and frustrating. Similarly, it is frustrating for both of you if some equipment necessary to complete a task is inaccessible to a child. For instance, if a child has been asked to help with the dusting, ensure that he can reach the polish or cloths.

Action! Try using the format suggested, and make more of your own. After a week or two, take time to discuss and assess what you have recorded. Do any patterns emerge? What time of the day is your child most receptive? Do the weather patterns affect the receptiveness of the child? What other factors seem to have bearing upon the child's willingness to concentrate on a task, or on your levels of patience?

What Is The Point Of All This?

A journal will assist you, the parent, to build up your own confidence.

Many parents who are new to home education or even considering it find the idea of teaching daunting: *"I don't know anything to teach him"*, *"I was useless at Science at school, I don't know any"*, *"I'm not a teacher, he won't learn anything from me"* are common fears. By keeping a journal in this way you may be surprised at the amount of knowledge which you do have, and the remarkable number of skills which you have surprised, not from school, but from your experience of life after school.

It will help you to get to know your child again.

When we first send our children into the reception class how quickly we lose touch with the people that we knew for the first few years of their lives! Even after a short period of schooling it will take time for you both to get to know each other again. It will also take time for you to get to know how your child thinks and how he learns - a vital clue as to what you can expect him to understand from now on.

In school, teachers should take time to get to know each child in a class, hence the introduction of baseline assessments which are supposed to aid this process. After a prolonged period of schooling both children and parents need to readjust to each other's ways, routines and expectations, and the simple action of writing a journal in this way will help you to focus your thoughts upon the needs of yourself and your child.

A journal gives written evidence of an ongoing education to the LEA.

Prior to their initial visit, which may be some months after you have taken the child out of school, this shows that you have not neglected their education, even if you have not embarked on a formal programme of study. Indeed, you may well choose not to do so on the basis of the evidence of an ongoing education which your journal provides.

Writing down what is happening on a day-to-day basis will give you the chance to question your own actions and form your own philosophy of what education really means. If you can justify whatever your child is doing and how much he is learning from doing it, you are providing an education, and you will be better equipped to argue your own case with authorities if challenged.

The journal will provide you with a record of probably the most significant phase of your child's life.

Writing a journal in this way can seem to be little more than a time-consuming chore, an additional job at the end of each day which a busy parent does not need. It can be seen as hard evidence for the LEA officers, but there are easier and more interesting ways of supplying this. Ultimately, the keeping of a journal even for a short time, will help you to see how much your child is learning without teaching. The very act of writing the journal will focus your attention upon the needs, interests and level of ability of your child and help you to get to know your own child again.

Start A Scrapbook

To supplement your own record, provide your child with a scrapbook in which they can put anything which will provide a record of their activities. This does not have to include writing, although any written work would be much appreciated by the LEA. Records and evidence can include pictures, photographs, objects which have been collected, newspaper cuttings, children's paintings and drawings - anything which will provide something to talk about or jog a memory. Do not forget to put a date when something is stuck in the scrapbook. If your child is unwilling to write even a title or heading for the pages of the scrapbook you might offer to do this for them.

The scrapbook constitutes an important record, so it must be looked after. Perhaps you could encourage your child to make an attractive cover for the book. Put it in a safe but prominent place, and encourage members of the family to take an interest in what has been produced by the child. Many children leave school with their confidence and self-esteem in tatters. Anything which can help to rebuild their feelings of self-worth must be encouraged, for as the child's confidence grows so will your own. Show your child that you value and treasure their creativity and you will be nurturing their holistic growth and education.

Deschooling

The people of every society are confronted by the problem of inducting the immature members into their culture, that is, into the ways of the group. The individual at birth is a cultural barbarian, in that he has none of the habits, ideas, attitudes and skills characterising the adult members of society...

In primitive societies the individual acquires these learnings informally from association with adults in their daily activities...In literate societies instruction in group ways becomes a partly specialised function. An institution - the school - is created.

Smith, Stanley and Shores 1957 - Cultural Diagnosis And The Idea Of A Common Culture Core Curriculum

While we would hesitate to suggest that home educators fall into the category of 'primitive' or illiterate societies, we do recognise the school as an institution. Other recognised institutions in our society include such places as hospitals, prisons and perhaps the services, where long-term association with a group or a confined space leads to the phenomenon of "institutionalisation".

 Institutionalisation:...to confine to an institution: as a result of such confinement, to cause to become apathetic and dependant on routine.

Chambers Dictionary

It is interesting that this condition is recognised as liable to cause problems to prisoners and long-term hospital patients, who are offered programmes of rehabilitation when they leave the institution. Members of the armed forces are offered similar courses of training, and long-term hostages are de-briefed, allowing them to work through awful experiences which they may have had. Counselling is often provided to workers upon their retirement, to assist them in adjusting to a new lifestyle. Schoolchildren, however, are not considered to be on a par with these groups, and they are expected to be able to cope without the habit or confinement of school immediately. Parents too have their lives and routine disrupted when children come out of school. This is compounded by the fear of inspection, the threat of legal action if no evidence of education can be produced, and the inability to cope with a child who appears to want to do nothing much but play or watch television. It appears from the dictionary definition, given above, that this apathetic behaviour is to be expected in those who have been part of an institution for some time. It is therefore hardly surprising when parents remark on how little children seem to do, or seem to wish to do when school ceases.

Children find school distressing for a variety of reasons. We read and hear a great amount about bullying in the media at the moment and certainly this is a major factor in the decision of many families to home-educate. Bullying can take many forms. It often comes from the child's peer group but frequently overlooked to the point of being almost expected is the amount of teacher/child bullying and even teacher/parent bullying which is evident in schools.

A significant number of home-educated children have problems with the work which they are asked to do in school. Perhaps it is too difficult, and they are afraid to ask for help. Sometimes help, when it is offered, is insufficient to solve the problem. Maybe time does not allow for the explanations to be given fully enough for the child to understand, or the pressures of timetabling and the need to achieve good results override the concerns for the needs of the individual.

Sometimes the work given is too easy. Children become bored and see no reason to continue attending lessons. Or they feel that the lessons of school have little or no relevance to life outside of school, their chosen career or their interests. The link to truancy and anti-social behaviour is obvious: *"The Devil finds work for idle hands"*. Whatever the reason for rejecting the school system, many children leave school emotionally, psychologically and sometimes physically damaged.

Where a child has found the experience of schooling difficult, or where he has been damaged in some way, it may well take some time for him to heal. It is estimated that in some cases deschooling a child can take as long as a year. Undoubtedly a child who has come through any bad experience at school will need some time for rest and recovery before they can face another piece of paper or pencil, or any hint of formal (possibly even informal) study. As parents you too will need time to adapt to a new way of life.

Time is a great healer, and does work. However healing is unlikely to take place if you, the parents, allow yourselves to be panicked into replicating school at home on that first fateful Monday morning.

Of course, home educators do not have the restrictions imposed by weekends or school holidays, or even 'working hours' between 9:00 and 3:15. If your students work better first thing in the morning, you may like to make an early start, and have the whole thing done by mid morning. Some children need frequent breaks, and some prefer to work straight through, taking a drink and a biscuit with them to their table.

Before imposing rules about how and when to work, what is acceptable and what is not, spend a few moments analysing the way in which you work, and questioning why schools impose some of the rules that they do. Do you, for instance, take a cup of coffee to the table when you sit to write a letter? Do you find that thinking is easier when you are weeding the flower beds, or playing a musical instrument? Do you sometimes need to go to a friend for a chat to sort out your own feelings or ideas, or to seek help with a problem? As adults, we often behave in a way which is considered unacceptable for children in school.

At school children are not allowed to move far from their desks for periods of up to 90 minutes. To go to the lavatory they need to ask permission, sometimes even written permission has to be sought. They must spend most of their school time maintaining silence, communication with others in the same room being kept to a minimum.

We at home can be, and should be, much more relaxed. If we expect children to learn to behave as reasonable adults then we should treat them as such. We expect them to take responsibilities in three particular ways:

Care Of Oneself

Each member of the family can be encouraged to take care of themselves and their possessions. As a general rule, do not do anything for a child which he can do for himself. Pre-school children can often dress themselves, needing help only with buttons, zips and laces. It will help you if the child has clothes which he can manage by himself, and give him a feeling of independence. Children can be shown how to take care of their clothes, putting clean clothes away, and dirty clothes in the laundry basket. If provided with a duvet instead of sheets and blankets, even young children can make their own beds every morning. And children should be taught to look after their own personal hygiene, to clean their teeth regularly and correctly, to brush their own hair, and to keep themselves clean.

Care Of Others

Whether helping younger brothers and sisters, assisting with the preparation of meals for the whole family or showing consideration for older, younger or less able people, the care of others can be encouraged in our own children. Care of other people was, until recently, the basis of a common code of conduct in public: good manners. It extended to able-bodied people giving up seats for more frail members of the community and doors being held open for people laden with shopping, or pushing a pram. The stronger would go out of their way to help the weaker. Much of this now seems to have disappeared; common courtesy is not so common now, and apparently offends the supporters of the movement of political correctness. Personally, we still consider it important and are gratified when strangers comment that our children are so well-mannered,

Courtesy begins in the home: seeing and responding to a need, helping others and, in return, being able to ask for and expect help when it is needed. An awareness of the needs of others and the appropriate responses can be actively encouraged with children at home.

Care Of The Environment

Care for the environment on a global scale takes the same awareness as care for the immediate environment - the home. Putting one's clothes away and making beds may seem a long way from the issues of global warming and ozone layers, but the difference in personal attitude is only very slight. Again, by raising awareness within the family at an early stage firm foundations are built.

Other Ways Of Learning

As has already been briefly discussed, learning is not dependent upon formal lessons, books and written work. In fact, to demand such study of a child who has recently come out of school may be counterproductive. This section explores the other ways in which learning can occur within the home and context of family life, and justifies why children who are receiving an education at home should be involved in what might be generally seen as mundane housework.

When children are at school and parents are working, whole families split up and go their separate ways each day. Home education has the opposite effect. In place of the usual fragmented regime, home education has the effect of bringing families more closely together. Some would claim that home education is a first line defence against the onset of ageism, as children educated at home are better equipped to socialise and work with people both older and younger than themselves.

Certainly, a common observation among home educators is the closeness of the family, lack of sibling rivalry and tolerance of different age groups.

The mere presence of other people in the house creates work for the person who is the home-maker. If that person is also assuming the role of home educator their work load triples. How are you going to manage?

If you have other people in the house all day you have a potential work force. After all, your children are not your guests, they are part of the family. Even young children can participate in the running of the home and assume some level of responsibility for themselves, for others and for their immediate environment. Is this such a bad idea? After all, one day the intention is surely that your brood will take to their wings and fly the nest, and that will surely be the test of your success as a home educator.

It is an alarming indictment of the school system in that it allows our young people to achieve high qualifications to secure a place at a university, but does not prepare them for life sufficiently to ensure that they are able to cook a simple meal or launder their own clothes when they get there. Television cooks have cashed in on this glaring gap in general knowledge to the extent that we are offered programmes featuring such skills as boiling water.

As home educators we have a stark choice. Either we take on a lot of extra work or we involve the children and do the chores together. As advocates of a holistic approach to education we definitely suggest developing the latter.

Children are able to help with household chores, cooking, cleaning and care of pets if they are adequately supervised and not put into any danger from household appliances or cleaning materials. Even the youngest love to help. The housework may take a little longer. The tasks of cleaning may not be executed as thoroughly as you might have wished, but consider how much will be gained from involving the children.

There will be opportunities for learning, discussion and conversation, and by involving them you will be contributing to their sense of self-esteem and developing their respect for you as a person rather than some kind of slave.

At the onset of home education, involvement in housework may be the only kind of learning which motivates a school-damaged child. Putting books, paper and pencils on the dining room table and expecting learning to take place may be at the very least counter-productive and possibly downright disastrous.

Learning Through Real Tasks

Housework

Even if the children are at home all day, the house needs to be organised and run as a home. Either more work is created when more people are in the house for prolonged periods, or the work is shared. There will be more cleaning, more cooking, and more washing-up to be done, not less! Shopping and housework require skills in organisation, planning and budgeting. These skills form part of a full time education which will prepare your child for life when he has to fend for himself.

By expecting children to take a full and active part in running the house, you will be providing real learning situations. Even a young child can help with household tasks, providing that he is safe and adequately supervised, and that the task is appropriate to the child's ability.

Washing-up can be fun, but sinks are hard for children to reach. Hot taps can be dangerous if the water is too hot for little hands. Most immersion tanks have a thermostat which can be turned down to a safe level. Check yours before letting a child loose in the kitchen or bathroom.

Cleaning jobs like dusting, polishing, vacuuming and mopping are not beyond the capabilities of most children, providing they are physically big enough to cope with any equipment. Not only will you get the house clean, but you will also provide the child with some physical exercise. Children love cleaning, especially if water is involved. Cleaning the bathroom is one of the most popular jobs in our house, and well within the capabilities of a child of seven. The usual precautions must be taken and children are to be taught the dangers of using household cleaning products. They should not be expected to handle dangerous substances like bleach, but it is not unreasonable to expect a child of junior school age to use bathroom cleaner.

Dealing with household cleaning materials is part of an all-round education. Children need to learn how to use products and machinery safely, as much as they need to learn how to cross a road. Giving a child work to do gives responsibility and independence. If you are dealing with your own child in a learning situation in your own home, you will be able to supervise much more closely and effectively than a stranger with a large group of children would.

Changing bed linen can be turned into a game, as can throwing it all down the stairs and putting it into the washing machine. Children often have a natural affinity with machines, and can quickly learn how to program a washing machine. Through sorting white washing from coloureds and woollens from other fibres children learn about fabrics and their different properties. At first you will need to be vigilant, and remind them to empty pockets and sort the washing carefully.

Preparing Food

The provision of food is another area where children can learn in a real situation. Involve the children in planning meals and take the opportunity to talk with them about nutrition. Cooking can become part of the everyday education at home, and children will soon learn quite advanced cooking techniques if they work alongside you in the kitchen.

Skills involved in cooking include chemistry, biology and hygiene, practical maths and reading. If you extend the study of foods bought each week, you could easily include geography, and comparing what is available now to a weekly shopping list even five years ago is a good starting point for historical study of food and economics.

Take a look at your kitchen equipment before embarking on cooking with your children. Scales are vital. A set of balances is a good tool for young children to weigh with, as they can see what is happening and can practice adding more or taking away from one side until a balance is achieved.

In schools metric measurements are used throughout. Two points should be noted, however:

i. When measuring in imperial units, the numbers involved are much more manageable for a young child. The weight of half a pack of butter is easily calculated if the pack is 8 ounces, but not if it is 250 grams.

ii. We have come across school-leavers who simply have no idea how long a yard is, nor how heavy a pound is. While we live within our current dual system it seems only fair to introduce both systems to our children.

Attention must be paid to safety in the kitchen. Knives, electrical equipment and hot surfaces are all potential hazards, and children should never be left unsupervised.

Involve your child in planning and budgeting for meals. Encourage him to take and active part in food preparation, cooking and serving family meals.

As more families eat in front of the television and fewer families have meals together, the skill of laying a table is one which we are in danger of losing. Mealtimes are invaluable social occasions, and laying the table is something which even members of the family as young as one year old can help with.

Putting cutlery in the correct place reinforces right and left for older children, as does using a knife and fork. Serving food and table manners can be taught by example, and clearing away demands organisation and planning.

Gardens

Every child should have the opportunity to grow something. If you have not got a garden, some seeds can be sown in a pot or window box, or house plants propagated on a window-sill. If you do have a garden, find a space which can be a child's own patch of ground.

Encourage children to grow plants and seeds, and allow them to help you in the garden. Skills involved with gardening include reading for information, science including basic chemistry and biology, awareness of seasons and temperature, weather and aspect, art, colour and design.

Lawnmowers and rotavators are definitely off limits for children. Watch out for chemicals used in gardening and for pest control, as they really can be dangerous.

Many schools keep classroom pets which children take turns to feed and clean. At home it is often possible to keep pets and, if so, much can be learned from caring for animals. If you are able to keep even one small creature for a child to love and tend it is a worthwhile experience. The child will need to know about the correct food to give a pet, measure the right quantity and feed the animal frequently enough, change and clean the bedding, and give the animal exercise and attention. A Cyberpet cannot replace experience with living creatures which cannot be switched off or thrown away.

If your child has a pet, hand over responsibility for the care of the animal to the child as far as possible. When children are free of school they have plenty of time available to feed, clean and exercise pets. If you do not have any pets, now is the time to consider getting one if possible. pets provide companionship, are a source of interest and nurture an attitude of responsibility.

Shopping

Home education has the marvellous advantage over school education because it provides the ideal opportunity for children to work in and experience the real world. Schools have to bring the real world in, often in some form of package - through books, IT, or visitors who will give a talk or a display. If an excursion is arranged it must be suitable for large groups and supervision for those groups must be provided. Home educators have no such restrictions.

A trip to the supermarket provides an opportunity for children to use a shopping list, compare prices, weigh and measure quantities, and learn about refrigeration. Encourage your children to pay for some shopping, and handle money. Persuade them to estimate the total cost of shopping in the basket, and to work out the amount of change which you will receive.

A walk round a familiar town or village can give no end of talking points. In this way, even a trip to the local shop can present a real and valuable opportunity for learning to take place. For example:

- Look above the shop fronts in your town, and finding first-hand historical evidence in the facades of the buildings.

- Look for patterns in the brickwork and tiling of the buildings.

- Discuss the styles and ages of buildings and street furniture.

- Observe new buildings which are under construction and talk about what is happening.

If you do not know an answer to a question that your child asks, find out the answer together with him. Do not be afraid to ask questions; if your child asks why people are digging up the road, go forward and ask them. Usually people are only too happy to stop working and show off their knowledge. Having got your answer, use it as a springboard to discuss with your child the services which are brought into our homes underground.

Preparing For The LEA's First Visit

Informal Learning

The emphasis so far has been on a very informal approach to learning based on everyday activities within and around the home. The only special efforts required on behalf of the parents at this time are to have patience allowing the child to work at his pace, to keep the diary, and to make an attempt at analysis of what is being learned, when and how. Parents are on a learning curve, too. Hopefully, the action of keeping a diary in this way will have enabled you to identify learning opportunities which exist, and to increase your confidence in your own skills and abilities. You should be able to trace back learning in the home to recognisable school curriculum subjects.

Many home educators see no reason to go much farther than this in the task of educating their own children. Others wish to have more in the way of a structure and identifiable timetable for home education. As your confidence as a home educator grows you may find, as many do, that in fact you move between having a structured timetabled approach and more informal learning. In either case, there is a need for some record of learning to be kept, together with some evidence in the form of written work, paintings and drawings, a scrapbook or diary made by the child. All such evidence should be clearly dated and named, as this will provide a record of progress for yourself and your child, and satisfy the LEA's requirements when they monitor the education which your child is receiving.

If you have deregistered your child from a school it is not unreasonable to expect to hear from the LEA within a few weeks of the child leaving school. In some counties an Education Welfare Officer may call within days, but normally this is only to confirm the names of the children who are no longer attending school, and to make some informal assessment of the seriousness of your intention to home-educate. The authorities have to give you a reasonable amount of time to establish a pattern of home education, and it is unlikely that you will be visited by an advisor within the first six weeks of leaving school. In most authorities it is considerably longer before a home visit is suggested.

An advisor will not necessarily expect to see a full programme of home education up and running. Usually, it is sufficient to show that:

i.   You have given due consideration to resolving problems at school and investigating alternatives to school before making the decision to home-educate. You have not taken this decision lightly.

ii. You have begun to develop your own philosophy of education, based upon knowledge of the law, the experiences of other home educators and an amount of research into the subject. You know what you want from education and what you reject

iii. You have made an initial attempt at observing and recording how your child learns, identifying his interests and skills, and assessing his level of understanding. You intend to use the information gathered in future planning of activities which will form the basis of home education. You have kept a detailed analytical journal since the child was deregistered from school, and are acting upon the information in it.

iv. There is some evidence of learning from the child. This does not have to be on paper - tape recordings, videos, photographs, craftwork etc. all count as evidence. Date any piece of work which your child produces and keep it safe.

v.   You have some idea as to how to proceed henceforth, and have some support - from your partner, friends and/or family, and have contact with other home educators, perhaps through a support group.

Sometimes it is at the first visit of the LEA advisor that new home educators are really put on the spot and need to have answers to a few questions regarding their motives. Naturally, many people find the visit a nerve-wracking experience, even when your visitor is kind, supportive and anxious to put you at ease. It is as well to remember that the LEA visitor is not going to be the only person who you will be answerable to - once you have announced your intention to home-educate, then friends, family, neighbours and total strangers will be asking for quite personal details as to how you are educating your child, and you will need to decide if and how to respond.

LEA home education managers have plenty to do - they seldom, in our experience, sit in their offices waiting for new home-educating families to appear in their 'in' trays, so the likelihood is that you will have some time to sort yourselves out. It may be a full school term before you are visited by the LEA manager for your area, and they do have to give you time to sort out your own lives and approach to home education before much can be demanded such as curriculum details and programmes of study.

Recording Children's Work

The LEA will want to see some evidence of an ongoing education, however, and need to be reassured that you are taking the whole matter of your child's education seriously. This does not necessarily mean that you will have to produce numerous exercise books, rows of sums and rows of ticks but something which is on paper, tape or film and which you can offer as evidence of education will be well received. If you have a camera or tape recorder, now is the time to make good use of it. Keep a copy of anything which your child puts on paper - writing, drawing, painting - and date it. It will be part of the file of evidence of an ongoing education which you will be able to show to the LEA home education manager when he visits.

Know your rights and do not be intimidated. The LEA's visit is not an examination of your ability to educate your child and they have no powers to 'pass' or 'fail' you. LEA officials may offer advice regarding the work which your child is doing but this is really only their opinion. You can take the advice given if you want to but it is not legally binding in any way. Be prepared, however, to justify the methods of education which you are using, and be prepared to discuss your plans for the future. The latter can be kept fairly open - circumstances may alter, or in the light of experience you may change your mind and plans. The LEA may appreciate seeing the records which you have kept so far, but these are for your personal use, and there is no reason for the LEA to have a copy.

As a home educator responsible for the education of your child, no one has the right to tell you what you should be studying or when. How you organise your time is entirely up to you, and whether or not you decide to follow the National Curriculum is also your decision.

If you are registered with the LEA the advisor may wish to visit you at regular intervals. He may seek assurance that you are

The role of the LEA is not to question the parent's right to remove his or her child from the school system in order to provide a different sort of education. The LEA must simply evaluate whether the education of youngsters is, in the words of the 1993 Education Act, "efficient and suitable to their age and aptitude", even though no watertight definition of any of these terms is available.
Richard Bates 'Education Otherwise: The LEA's Role In Home Education.'

providing a balanced curriculum; that is, not ignoring any subject area completely. How you accomplish that is up to you and the LEA cannot be depended upon for any guidance on this matter.

Home Education Is Not Home Tuition

It comes as a shock to some parents who, having deregistered their child from school, expect that the LEA will arrive ready to give help, advice and guidance, if not to provide a professional home tutor. Home tuition is only available to children who are unable to attend school on the grounds of health. A letter from a GP stating that this is the case is a necessary prerequisite before home tuition will be considered by the LEA. Even if home tuition is granted, it is likely to be considered a temporary measure, and the child is expected to return to a school sooner or later. Home tuition is very different from home education, and the two should not be confused.

Preparation

It is not in the remit of the LEA to advise a home-educating family on how to design a home education package, where to find resources, or how to teach specific skills. The LEA may be quick to tell you if they do not like what they see, but they will not necessarily tell you in any detail what they DO want to see.

The clearer you are in your own mind what you see as constituting an education and the better you understand your rights in terms of the law, the better placed you will be to answer the LEA's questions:

- Read the chapter relating to the law, work through the exercises concerning the development of your own educational philosophy, and keep a home education journal.

- Discuss your observations, thoughts and ideas with a trusted friend, meet with other home educators and read around the subject.

- Arm yourself with knowledge, become your own expert and be ready to justify your actions with confidence.

- However you and your child choose to study, keep all the work which your child has done clearly marked with the date, as this will help the LEA in their job.

- A reading list and good records of the work your child has covered can also be important, especially if home education is a stop-gap or transitory solution and your child intends to return to school.

In time, you may change your mind or modify your ideas, and of course, you are allowed to do so. For the time being, however, it is important that you are able to show that you take the matter of your child's education seriously, and that you have the right to be taken seriously by anyone who should enquire.

The Visit Of The LEA Advisor

The advisor cannot demand entry to your home, and should not turn up unannounced; he should make an appointment at a mutually convenient time. It is usual for the advisor to visit you in your home, but if you do not want this to happen, say so when you reply to their letter. They should be able to make alternative arrangements. It is not your home which is being inspected, but the educational provision which you are making for your child. The LEA visit, especially the first one, is often an anxious time for home educators. No one enjoys being tested, inspected or criticised by an official, and the thought of the visit can strike fear into the hearts of even the most experienced home educators. Before continuing with how the visit of the LEA can be approached, let us spare a thought for the LEA advisor, and try to see the situation from his point of view.

What Do LEA Advisors Do?

LEA advisors are as isolated, if not more so, as home-educating families can be. These people often have other responsibilities as well as home education. When their sole responsibility is monitoring home educators, they are generally employed for only one or two days a week. Most come to the job with little or no knowledge about home education, and few are offered any training. When training is given, it appears to be in the form of shadowing an EWO or advisor for a day, and becoming acquainted with the legality of home education - the training period may only last for a few hours. Many advisors receive no training at all. Many remain ignorant of the law or put their own interpretation upon it.

Few authorities have more than two advisors, usually only one who is responsible for monitoring. They work in isolation within the authority, and with little contact with advisors in other authorities. They have no guidelines from the DfEE on how to perform their function, and very little guidance internally. The normal practice is simply to continue with the previous advisor's policy, thus generating something of a folk culture.

The first contact an advisor has with a new home-educating family is likely to be when a formal notification of deregistration from the school lands in the in-tray. Equipped with your name and address and the details of your child's name and age, the advisor then may send a standard form to you. These forms may have been designed up to ten years ago. Any written guidelines might have been revised after the 1996 Act, or there may be no guidelines in place. In fact, there may be no clear written policy on home education, and in a significant number of LEAs, there is some confusion as to who, if anyone, is responsible for home education. The form is dispatched, and it is not until it has been completed and returned to the office that a visit might be arranged. Failure to complete the form will probably result in a visit from an EWO, who will want assurance regarding the welfare of the child. The LEA will not simply vanish if you ignore them.

When the completed forms have been received from you, the LEA advisor will write to suggest a time and date when a visit could take place. The tone of the letters will vary, and it is often presented as a *fait accompli* where the home educator has little choice in the matter. Let us imagine, however, that you agree to see the advisor in your home at the time suggested.

On that day the advisor will arrive at your address, knowing only your name and the name of the deregistered child. He will probably be alone, very rarely they are accompanied by an EWO. The advisor will not know how he is going to be received, nor how successful his visit will be in achieving its aims. He has very little power - he cannot demand entry, insist on seeing the child or expect to check the child's work. He is there on your terms. He is in a vulnerable position and probably experiences as much stress and anxiety as the home educator.

Seeing fly-on-the-wall documentaries about other families and other lives on television can never equip us for the shock of the reality of other people's situations. Not everyone's home is like your home: not everyone's values are like your own. Seeing another family's home and way of life can generate any emotion from envy to disgust, awe to pity. The advisor setting out for the first home visit may find the address leads to a mansion or a hovel; when he knocks on the door it might be opened by a deferential butler or an abusive aggressor.

The advisor is going into an unknown situation in an unfamiliar place and needs to make contact with a family who he has never met before. He is aware that he is likely to be seen as someone who represents authority, and that he may not be well received. He is also aware that he has no powers to do his job, and he goes unaccompanied. How would you feel if it were you? How would you wish to be received?

The point to be made here is that at the time of the initial visit there is a degree of stress and fear on both sides. As has already been discussed, fear is often a destructive and unhelpful emotion, and causes people to behave in irrational, sometimes aggressive, ways. Home educators and LEAs often become so fearful of each other from the onset that it is almost impossible to build any sort of constructive co-operative relationship. This is a shame, for it may be that each side has something of value to contribute to what must be acknowledged as the ultimate aim - securing the best education possible for a child.

How To Handle The Visit

As a home educator you have a number of choices regarding the visit. As far as the venue is concerned you could:-

i.   Refuse to have a home visit or to meet with the LEA advisor, but offer to provide evidence of the education of your child and put some copies of samples of work covering the period during which the child has been out of school in the post. This should satisfy the requirements of the law.

ii. Refuse to be visited at home, but offer to meet the advisor at their office or at a mutually convenient venue, e.g. the local school. This paves the way for a constructive relationship in the future, and allows the LEA advisor to see that you are serious about home education, open to constructive criticism, and acquainted with your rights.

iii. Agree to the visit taking place in your home.

Having settled the venue, you could resolve to comply with all the demands of the advisor. Alternatively, you might make sure you are aware of your rights and the rights of your child, and whilst making every effort to be friendly, open and welcoming, keep the visit on a fairly formal basis, writing down what is said for your own records.

On The Day Of The Visit

This section assumes that you are proceeding with a home visit from the LEA advisor.

All home educators are different, just as all advisors are different, and all LEAs are different. There is no standard prescription for coping.

We ourselves are fortunate in living in an area with a well-informed advisor who is highly supportive of home-education. From some families who have contacted us we hear horror stories of offensive advisors who transgress their authority, so making it tricky to develop a constructive relationship. It is to be hoped that by diplomatic means the situation can be improved but, whatever does happen, it is important to be fully aware of your legal rights and responsibilities.

In general, when the advisor arrives, you should be friendly and co-operative. Make your visitor welcome, but keep on formal terms, with title and surname rather than forename.

Unless there is good reason not to, offer the child's work for inspection. The room in which you talk to the advisor could show evidence of activity, for example with the child's pictures on the walls. Listen to what the advisor says and make notes of any significant points. If you have joined a support group, let the advisor know.

Be confident. Make sure the advisor is aware that you know what you are doing and can justify your actions. Do not be afraid to express an opinion. Avoid the topic of school, though. It is behind you now.

We encourage our children to make the tea or coffee, to serve it and hand round biscuits. This has the effect of demonstrating to the advisor the child's confidence, ability and manners and it also impresses upon the child that the advisor is important. In addition, the way has been cleared for easy communication between the advisor and the child.

Treat the advisor's visit as you would any other official visit, such as that of the insurance man, the doctor or the meter reader. Finally, thank him for coming and express your willingness to co-operate in the future.

As has already been discussed, only children who have been deregistered from state schools are automatically known to the authority. Being registered as a home educator does mean that you will be subject to monitoring, and this can be rather tiresome. Being known to the authorities does have some advantages, however. It is more difficult for anyone to accuse your child of truancy, for example, if a telephone call to the LEA will be able to confirm that they are home-educated. When dealing with other people this can be a distinct advantage, and perhaps needs to be borne in mind with the advent of so very many security CCTV systems in shops and town centres. The Truancy Act which came into force 1st December 1998 empowers the police working with the Education Welfare Service to detain any known truants, so it is increasingly important that home-educated children can be identified and protected.

Attitudes Of Other People

In any social interaction we are frequently met with anything from fascination to dismay as a reaction. What is always apparent is people's interest; a child's education is an important aspect of parenthood and there are many people who would at least consider an alternative to state education. Be prepared to talk about it.

"I don't go to school"

"I knew it! That's just what this town needs - another ignoramus!"

Children's film - "Pete's Dragon"

In Chapter 3 we looked at frequently asked questions. They really are asked frequently, and you will find yourself repeating the same stock phrases to many acquaintances. Make sure, then, that you can give a confident answer to each. One home-educating family made their own leaflets describing their style of education which they hand out freely to all that enquire.

Emotionally, education is a highly-charged subject. There are few natural forces stronger than that of the protection and nurturing of offspring by the parent. It is no surprise, then, to observe the defensive attitude of a schooled child's parent when faced with the (probably new) concept of home-education. Unacceptable is any hint that he has not done the best for his child.

Some home educators find it difficult to talk to others about their choice to home-educate. This is understandable, as home educators are prone to criticism, often harsh, especially from members of their own families. By the time you and your children are out and about in the local town during school hours, you may be feeling very defensive. Remarks like, *"No school today, then?"* from well-meaning shopkeepers send some home educators scuttling out of the shop, muttering something about teaching them at home. By being frank when explaining to people who have remarked on the children not being in school, the reaction has been surprisingly positive - often along the lines of *"I wish I had..."*, or *"I know someone else who does..."*, or *"Are you allowed to? I know someone who wants to and she doesn't know where to begin..."*

The child's own parents are the ones to experience the negative side of schooling first-hand. We are the ones who have to deal with rebellious, unhappy, frightened children, it is we who get them to school each day, and cope with their nightmares and bedwetting. Many of us take the decision to home-educate when all else has failed. Home education means choosing to make sacrifices, but we are prepared to do this for the sake of our children's happiness and well-being. One mother was aware that by choosing home education she would have to give up her full-time job, and they would have to move to a smaller house, but as she said, *"I'd do anything, make any sacrifice, if my son were happy and learning something."*

It is both hurtful and confusing when other family members are severely critical of your decision to home-educate. When you have the best interests of the child at heart, why does the decision to home-educate cause others such anguish?

First, home education is still relatively new and uncommon in this country. The implication is of pushy, over-ambitious parents or unruly children who have been excluded from school. Home education can be a source of embarrassment for relatives who have to admit that the children are being taught at home, and may be put into the position of having to justify that when they are not certain of the reasons, the legality, or the positive sides of home education themselves.

Secondly, there is still a good deal of uncertainty surrounding home education. *"How can you teach physics?"*, *"What about his GCSEs"*, *"What about the social side of school?"* - these are questions and criticisms which are often voiced, especially from the older generation. Even when our answers show that in fact we have thought about all these so-called problems and dealt with them, the family remain doubtful and unconvinced.

"...the major criticism home educators face from relatives, friends and acquaintances...curiously, does not concern academic progress or the ability of untrained parents to educate their children at home. Rather it is that children will be deprived of social contact with peers and lack experience in the real world outside the home.

...some...suggest that it is school which is not in the real world and that the institutional nature of schooling, along with restrictive peer culture, may actually impede and distort healthy social development."
Alan Thomas, Educating Children At Home

When dealing with people and relatives outside the immediate family we are in the business of educating not only our own children but all other interested parties too. The same rules apply as with education of children - all we need to do is to facilitate a learning situation, so allowing the most effective learning to take place. Effective learning does not come from instruction, so there is little point in having an *"Oh yes I can!"* *"Oh no you can't"* discussion about the merits of home education with someone who has not yet reached a stage in their personal development when they can accept that there is more than one way of doing anything. Two and a half thousand years ago Socrates had discovered this truth, and his teaching methods consisted mainly of asking skilful questions which led the enquirer to discover the answers for themselves.

Sometimes, then, the most effective tactic is to listen politely and to say as little as possible, asking the critic questions, rather than giving defensive answers. You may well face sweeping and unfounded claims, such as, *"your children won't be able to socialise with others their age"* or *"children who don't go to school do not have the skills to cope with the rough and tumble of life"*, Respond by challenging your interlocutor to back his statement with evidence. We are quite confident that this challenge will not be met! We have yet to find any research or documentation on home education which backs these statements, or negates the success, quality or effectiveness of home education.

> *...Of course, it must be possible for home education to be a failure, but I just have not come across any cases.*
> **R. Meighan, Learning From Home Education.**

Summary

This chapter has addressed the ways in which new home educators can expect to be questioned about their approach to education, their responsibility and qualifications for the job, and suggested ways of dealing with these questions. The questioning does not cease - for as long as you home-educate and probably beyond, people will question you about your decision, its wisdom and its effects. We may tire of answering the same questions over and over, but it is the price of being interesting. As Malcolm Muggeridge said, *"only dead fish swim with the stream"*.

Chapter Seven

Towards Autonomy - A Scheme For Study

Home is where one starts from. As we grow older
The world becomes stranger, the pattern more complicated...

TS Eliot, East Coker

A New Word

The dictionary gives definitions for all sorts of words close to that of the parent/educator/mentor/guide, but none accurately describe the whole role, and some have unsuitable connotations and associations. We therefore bring in a new word - wissian. In fact, it is not new, it is the Anglo-Saxon for a *guide*, but we introduce it as a word that has no hidden agenda, with a definition:-

Wissian - one who aids in the education of a child, whether through knowledge, instruction, guidance, encouragement or provision of resources.

Comparing Schooling With Home Education

School provides children with a rigid regime in which learning can take place. The movements and activities of children in school are governed by the clock - a result of strict timetabling and management which is necessary to operate any large organisation. In schools it is especially important to know where any child is at any particular time, as a point of safety as much as ensuring an adequate education is being received.

> `But we don't WANT to teach 'em,' replied the Badger. `We want to LEARN 'em—learn 'em, learn 'em! And what's more, we're going to DO it, too!'
> **Kenneth Grahame, The Wind In The Willows**

A home education can be much more flexible as it is more relaxed. Of course, it is important to know where each child is and what they are doing, and sometimes an activity may need to have a time limit imposed, but home educators do not have to work in lessons, have regular breaks of fifteen minutes when everyone stands outside, or stop an interesting activity when the bell rings. We are not governed by weekdays or school terms - learning is a year-round process, and breaks occur naturally, if at all.

How to achieve the transition from school to home education can be difficult for parents to see, so much so that many are put off and revert to schooling even though they feel that it is not right for them or the children. If a child is accustomed to school life and school holidays, there may well be a need for a debriefing period during which time they can get used to the notion of working at home on school-type tasks. Parents as well often need some help in planning tasks and organising time, and this is what the scheme of work in this book describes.

The method of working which is described in this chapter bridges the gap between the rigours of a school regime and a completely autonomous child-led approach to home education. It is intended to ensure that each child receives an all-round education through a balanced curriculum, has individual tuition time each day, has time when he is expected to work on his own, and has opportunities for the real work of running a home.

This describes a particularly structured approach to working. As you become increasingly proficient at teaching your child and more relaxed about home education, you may find that you wish to ease up on many aspects of this approach to work, and of course you are free to do so. Conversely, it may be that you feel the need for a structure to work, and like the security of the system. As your child grows, you may wish to add other subject areas, or take out others, and the scheme allows for flexibility in this way. There is no right way of approaching the education of any individual. If it works and you are happy with it, use it.

One of the main attractions of opting for a home education is that, unlike schools, no curriculum is imposed. Restrictions which schools place upon movement of children, methods of learning and resources and time available to study are no longer significant impediments when home is the base for learning. Education can be autonomous, that is, designed around and fulfilling the needs of each individual child. The idea of autonomous education is not a new one. It was first documented in the philosophies of the Ancient Greeks. More recently, in the 18th and 19th Centuries writers like Rousseau and John Dewey influenced educational thinking and reform. The notion of individual learning was embodied in the Plowden report 1967.

Autonomous learning does not translate to 'do whatever you like, whenever you like', to the exclusion of the adult responsible. That is neither fair to the child, the family who live with the child or the society in which he lives - no attempt is made to interfere with the child's natural development, no correction is given and no examples are set. Autonomous education does not exclude suggestion from others as to how a learner might develop his ideas or use the knowledge which he has acquired in order to move forward in his understanding of the world around him. This forward movement, facilitated by the wissian, is the basis upon which the individual educational strategy is constructed. True autonomous learning is an empowering concept. To be effective it requires a structure, it involves efficient management of time and resources, it demands intelligent learner-management and it uses all of the senses, rejecting nothing which may add to that learning.

A book on autonomous learning and home-based education has recently appeared. *'Doing It Their Way'* by Jan Fortune-Wood is published by Educational Heretics Press.

Successful Autonomous Education

A pattern of *observation-action-reflection* is recognised by researchers, typically by gathering data, analysing it and then drawing conclusions. The pattern is cyclic - after reflection comes more observation. Taken down to its bare bones, we have the simple, and repeating, formula:-

Watch - Do - Think

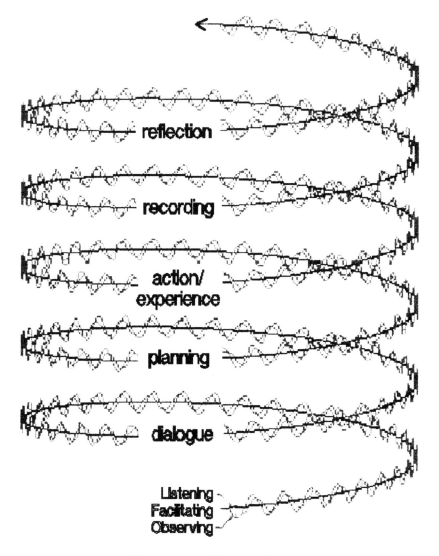

reflection

recording

action/
experience

planning

dialogue

Listening
Facilitating
Observing

Figure 3: Cyclic Learning

This is how learning occurs, naturally and effectively. Learning in this way continues throughout life. The model in Figure 3 illustrates this cyclic learning. As home educators, it is the task of the wissians to facilitate the cycle of dialogue, planning, action/experience, recording and reflection, but they are not working in isolation, or in an authoritarian role in this task. A large part of the responsibility for this lies with the child. The skills of listening to and observing the child are intertwined with the task of facilitating learning, as it is only through determining the needs and interests of the child that the appropriate experiences and action can be taken. Direct questioning - "What do you want to do?" - is unlikely to work; young children and disaffected children often do not know what they want to do. The answer is likely to be a rather flat "*Dunno*" or "*Nothing*". Rely on this method and autonomous home education may enjoy a very brief career. Establishing autonomous education needs to be democratic.

As a baby develops language another dimension to learning is added - that of communication. When a child learns to read and write another pathway to learning opens, and today computer literacy can be added to the list of ways in which communication can take place. Equipping children with these skills is a major concern of home-educating parents, and rightly so.

Parents do not flinch from the task of teaching their own babies language, in fact, listening and talking with a child who is learning to speak is often remembered by parents as one of the most delightful phases of a child's growing up. Yet language is arguably the most complex skill that will be learned in life. As a child grows, reading, writing, numeracy, knowledge of the arts and sciences are also necessary if he is to develop to his maximum potential as an educated adult and take his own place within society. For parents to disregard these areas of knowledge completely, adopting a policy of *the child will find out without any interference from me* could be argued as being irresponsible.

For example, the baby who is not given a cot toy in the first place is hardly likely to find out about sound and motion, or to develop skills of co-ordination. The weaker members of society, including the children, depend on the stronger for nurture and support. To deprive a baby of toys would invite accusations of cruelty. It is difficult to understand, then, how an approach to home education which rejects any suggestion of what to learn about and how to organise the learning, and which excludes any facilitation of learning can be justified. Autonomous learning firmly rejects coercion (*do as I say because I say so*), but it does not exclude suggestion as an initial stimulus, provision of information as motivation, or instruction as a tool through which skills can be acquired.

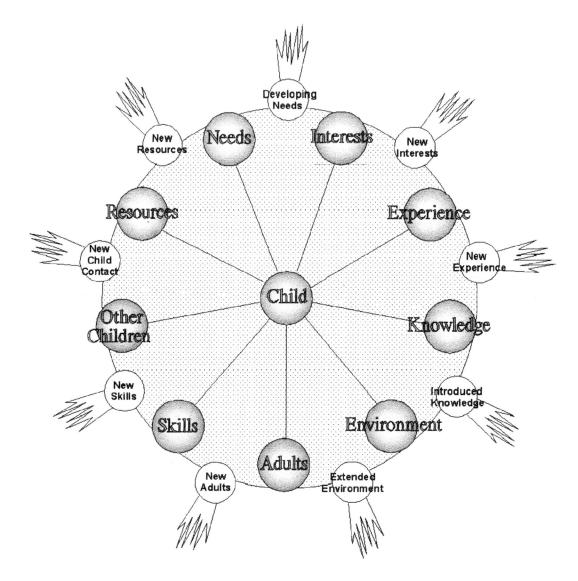

Figure 4: The Solar System

The model in Figure 4 illustrates the way in which the child directs his learning. The model is familiar - a diagrammatic portrayal of the solar system. At the centre of the model is the child. In his orbit are nine defined resources which he has to draw upon for his education - the 'planets of experience':-

The *Environment* is the surroundings in which he lives. The adults in his life - parents, extended family, established friends and neighbours, teachers, etc.. Through contact with adults he learns social skills, language, behaviour patterns and much more. He learns to survive in his home environment, wherever that may be. Rules for survival need to be learnt at an early age and adhered to. Quickly the child learns:

- don't touch the fire!

- don't play near the water!

- don't touch the medicines in the cupboard!

The *knowledge* which he has accumulated to date can be built upon. This refers to given knowledge - what he has been taught.

The *experience* a child has contributes to the wider body of knowledge, but it has not been acquired through direct instruction or teaching, but discovered by the child as an action/reaction phenomenon.

Interests refers to the natural inclination which any individual has for a specific subject area. Who can say why children develop an interest in any given subject? The fact is, they do have individual interests and learning takes place within the boundaries of those areas of interest.

Everyone has basic *needs* to survive. A child learns to request food if he is hungry, to ask for a bed if he is tired. Beyond physical needs he has the need to be loved and respected as an individual. As he grows and develops his needs extend to a desire for company of his age group and a search to acquire further knowledge.

Resources at his disposal for learning include everything and everybody within his immediate realm of experience. He will ask questions of the people he has had contact with, explore his world to the full and in his quest for knowledge he will demand answers and explore ad infinitum.

Other children provide resources for learning which adults cannot. His age group is available to be learned from, mimicked and to give explanations which he can often understand better than those given by adults. Children playing with other children give each other time which adults are unable to provide, so stimulating learning on a different level.

Skills are learnt and refined through contact with other planets of experience. Each skill can be developed to its limit within the realm of experience.

Adults provide security and company, and can facilitate learning through dialogue, example, experience and instruction.

All of the above provide a sound basis for learning, and for the young child knowledge gained from the immediate realm of his experience can be sufficient; in fact we could argue that little further input is necessary for young children. They need a secure realm of experience to be established before too much new information is introduced. Too much, too young is apt to confuse and distress a child.

For the home educator, the task is to broaden the realm of experience. Continuing to provide little more in terms of experience than has been given to a young child is insufficient. The job of the wissian is to introduce new experiences - the *comets of opportunity* - into the realm of the child.

New resources arrive naturally throughout life. Occasionally the opportunity to meet other people, to travel or to experience something new may arise. These opportunities arrive comet-like, injecting themselves into the realm of the child. Sometimes the new experience may have a passing acquaintance with the child, be there and gone like a comet in orbit, not to return for many years, if ever. Other opportunities may fall into the gravitational pull of our sun, the Child, who wishes to relive the experience or retain the resource for longer. For example, a parent may introduce a specialist teacher when a child wishes to learn a musical instrument. Perhaps the teacher and child do not form a good relationship, or perhaps the interest in the instrument is transitory, and both teacher and instrument are rejected. They go on their way, but the *experience* however brief, has still left an impression upon the child. He can add something to his library of knowledge, and at some future time the opportunity may present itself again. Equipped with the knowledge gained from experience the child may wish to have another try with the instrument, the teacher or both, or he is free to reject the opportunity again if he so desires. Either way, these *comets of opportunity* project themselves into our lives naturally, and always affect us.

The task of the wissians is to introduce 'comets of opportunity' to the experience of the child. They do not have to control the opportunities, simply to introduce them, wait, watch and act upon the response of the child. To leave this to chance is not enough. That is leaving education to chance, not taking the responsibility for it happening.

Structured Autonomy

Rejection of a failing system is easy, but suggesting what to replace it with is much more difficult. As home educators we have rejected the system offered at school, but to remove that and replace it with chance or nothing may equally fail our children.

It may seem strange, in a book advocating autonomous education out of school, to find included diagrams and charts which, at first glance, bear great resemblance to a school timetable. Look more closely. No times are given, no days are given. These charts suggest a means of managing time, ensuring that all the learner's senses are employed in the activity of learning, and that the basic tools of learning are provided through practice and teaching.

The structure described is not prescriptive. It can be used as printed, but we believe that home education is an organic process and will develop and change with time and experience, according to the needs of individual families. The emphasis is on democracy. The child decides what to learn, and when and how to learn it. The wissian provides the structure, thus ensuring that in the process of pursuing a line of enquiry, the basic building blocks of the child's education are not ignored.

The use of a structured approach in the early stages of home education is intended to empower the learner and to foster learner-management. It is an exercise in time-management and in achieving balance in education. It gives the grounding upon which learners can organise further study. It is intended to assist learners in working towards an effective autonomous, learner-management which is a skill in its own right, and one which is useful throughout life. As children grow, as greater responsibility is given and greater expectations are made, knowing how to use the tools of learning, to manage time and to prioritise activities, becomes much more significant.

Sooner or later the rug is pulled from under the learner, the infrastructure of prescribed lesson times and homework vanishes. It is often a rude awakening to students in their first year of university that there is no one to tell them how to organise their pattern of study - hence familiar tales of students who spend a disproportionate amount of time in the pub or partying, finding themselves in grave danger of being thrown out of college when assignments are missed.

It seems hardly right for the wissian to make plans for a learner-managed structure. Yet without the plans there is no structure. We are back to the *Watch-Do-Think* cycle, this time in the part of the wissian who must watch the child, evaluate the success of the plan and then allow time to reflect on the course of events. To review on a weekly basis would not be inappropriate when starting out.

What you learn through this process, and what your child learns, will determine the next action to be taken. It is inappropriate for home educators to attempt to provide long-term plans as teachers do in schools. The home education curriculum can be life itself, and as such it is unpredictable and dynamic.

> *"... it was the children themselves who insisted we create more structure and organisation in their education ... demanding 'timetables'; 'school holidays' and 'proper' work!"*
> **Cara Martin 'The Holistic Educators'**

What To Do And How To Do It

These two questions embody the provision of the school curriculum. The prescribed curriculum of the government tells teachers in some detail what to do and how to do it for any given age range of children. By following the prescription the children should be able to pass the given tests at the end of any Key Stage. Regular assessment and testing ensure that everyone is kept on track and provides teachers and parents alike that the educational provision (according to central government) is happening for each and every child in school.

It does not necessarily follow that home education is a rejection of the standards which have been set in schools. Home educators can, if they wish, follow the National Curriculum and the guidelines on delivery of the Literacy and Numeracy Hours. Details of the National Curriculum can be obtained from the local library, and are available from the Internet. If, however, you have rejected school because of the type of education which is prescribed on the National Curriculum, the twin problems of what to do and how to do it arise again.

Experienced home educators and researchers into the subject frequently advocate what has been termed as autonomous education. This is more than learner-managed learning, where parents pick up the cue from the skills and interests of their child, and a package of home education is developed around the experiences of the child. To reach the level of effective autonomous learning takes time and practice.

> *Whether it's popular or not doesn't come into it. It is on the curriculum. Everyone does it.*
> **Instructions from a Headteacher, on the subject of a Country Dancing lesson**

It is unlikely that a child who has been removed from school will have the skills to know what he is interested in, or what he does want to learn about. Schools, after all, are not in the business of justifying learning through enjoyment or personal interest. Any enjoyment derived along the way is via the relationship with the teacher. Personal interest in the prescribed curriculum is coincidental.

By the time a disaffected child has been deregistered from school and even after a period of 'rest and recovery', any attempt at coercion is unlikely to lead to a happy learning situation at home. The only starting point for many children is their own interests. the period of time after deregistration when you and your child are becoming deschooled and reacquainted with each other presents the opportunity for you to become aware of your child's own needs, interests and skills. By identifying these, you have the basic building blocks for a home education which will match the needs of the child, rather than yourself or the government.

A Topic-Based Approach To Learning

Our scheme works through exploration of a topic. By studying one topic in detail all eight subject areas of the recognised school curriculum can be covered. There are several advantages to working in this way with home students:-

It is no matter what you teach them [children] first, any more than what leg you shall put into your breeches first.
Samuel Johnson

- All aspects of study are linked to one central theme.

- Links can be made across the different subject areas, making study more relevant and producing an integrated curriculum.

- A single outing to a place of interest can provide material and inspiration for several weeks' work in all aspects of study.

- Children quickly see an application for the study of subjects in the curriculum as they can be related to a real situation.

- Opportunities for a learner-managed approach to education can be created in which the child's interests are central to the design of the learning plan.

- A planned topic provides security for new home-educating parents and evidence of educational provision for LEAs.

Choosing A Topic

As previously discussed, starting with an established interest stands more chance of success than beginning with a subject which is completely new and unfamiliar. By observing and listening to your child his interests will become apparent, and a suitable topic will emerge.

Perhaps, for example, you have a child who enjoys swimming, likes helping you in the garden and with cooking, and has an interest in animals. A general topic which encompasses some learning from all of these interests and brings in a few more leads can provide a starting point. Search for a common factor in the interests - in this case WATER might be a suitable topic title, as all the child's interests involve dealing with water in some form. Choose a topic which is specific, yet wide enough to bring in all areas of the curriculum as you see it and uses both factual and skill-based learning.

It may be very difficult to motivate a disaffected child damaged by the school system. By attaching the topic to a specific interest of his, for example horses, dinosaurs or space, you will increase your chance of achieving inspiration.

Designing A Topic Web.

Production of a topic web is the result of a brainstorming exercise which can involve as many members of the family who wish to participate. It begins with identification of and agreement on a subject which is of interest, incorporates specific topics which have been identified through dialogue with the child, and for which resources are available. The topic is often influenced by the season over which study is to take place. For instance, a topic like *Water* or *Gardens* is particularly relevant in the summer months, when children are likely to be outside in the fine weather, have the opportunity to visit the seaside or work in the garden, and gain first-hand practical experience of the topic which can be developed and extended. Autumn, on the other hand, provides an opportunity for exploring a topic like *Festivals*, as many cultures and religions celebrate feast days at this time of the year. It is also an opportune moment to consider such topics as seed distribution, fires, light etc.

When a general topic has been agreed upon, start the brainstorming exercise, each person contributing questions or ideas linked to the central theme which might form the basis for further exploration. Begin by making a list:

WATER		
What do we use it for?	Why do icebergs float?	Where does it come from?
Why does some tap water taste better than others?	Why do we buy water in bottles?	Why does it make a tinkling sound?
What makes bubbles?	What are rainbows?	Why is it wet?
Where does water go when we pull the plug out?	Why do rivers go faster in the middle than at the sides?	What is fluoride, and why is it put into water?
What makes waves happen?	Tell me about tides	What are water colours?
Why is there always a drop on the end of the tap which doesn't fall off?	Why do we have to pay for water?	Why did the soap froth up more when we went on holiday to Devon?

Figure 5: Brainstorming

The initial result of our brainstorming raised a number of diverse questions all of which are related to water. Analysis of them, however, puts most if not all, in the category of Science. Questions are, naturally, science based. If we stick to this model we might find some interesting answers, but the areas of Art, Language and Music will be in danger of being neglected. To ensure that all areas are covered, to facilitate whole-brain learning, building the Arts side of the curriculum into the study web is crucial at the planning stage. Perhaps the question which would produce a more open response in the first place is *Where do we find water?* These are the answers we came up with in five minutes:

In the tap	In ponds	In rivers	Underground
Fountains	Indoor fountains	In drinks	In food
In ourselves	In the sea	In the bird cage	In the garden
In the sky	In the fire-engines	In car engines	In radiators
Swimming pools	Water paints	In stories	In pictures
In music	In a car wash	In the bathroom	In pipes

Figure 6: Where do we find water?

Action! Use the next five minutes to add more of your own.

Take each answer in turn and ask further questions, and think of some activities which you could try to find the answers to your questions. For example:

In the tap - How does it get there? What is it used for - cooking, cleaning, drinking, washing? Where does it come from? What makes it hot or cold?

In fountains - Where do we find fountains? What are they for? Talk about different kinds of fountains. What sound do they make? Describe a fountain in words. Draw or paint a picture of a fountain. Photograph a fountain.

In stories - Find some stories with water in. Read or listen to the stories. Talk about the stories - how has the writer used the theme of water, and how have they used words to describe the water? Write or tell your own story or description of water.

In cars - Why do we put water in cars? Where do we put the water? What happens inside the engine? What does the water do? Why do we need to keep putting water in the engine - where does the water go? How much water does a car need? How do we measure water?

In ourselves - Where is water in our bodies? What happens to the water we drink? Why do we need to drink water? How much water does one person need? What percentage of our bodies is water?

Action! Continue with your own list and when you have done this, start to put each question in the list under one of the following headings - Number, Science, Geography, History, Language, Art, CDT, Music

---

There will be gaps, probably in the subject areas which you know least about. Music, for example, may need more research, perhaps by taking a trip to the record library or scanning the radio listings for Radio 3 or Classic FM to look for music with *water* in the title or theme. The act of researching

---

to fill in the gaps, however, expands your own knowledge and widens your own horizons. With a subject like music there is no need to have any knowledge of written music or to be a musician to listen and enjoy it. Remember, home is not school - you can put some music on in the background while another activity is going on, and it does not have to be restricted to classical music. This is multisensory learning, It is worth making an effort to find different music on the theme, unless, of course, you actually want to listen to *Raindrops Keep Falling On My Head* for six weeks.

There will probably be areas where the list of questions is too long. Not all of them need to be explored - just choose the ones which sound most interesting, or for which you know you can get some resources or visits to back up study. Overall, aim for about six different questions in each subject area. Our sample study web is shown on page 138. Use it as a basis for designing your own, add to it and take out ideas. Most of all, make full use of your own unique interests, skills, resources and facilities, as these will form the basis of learning.

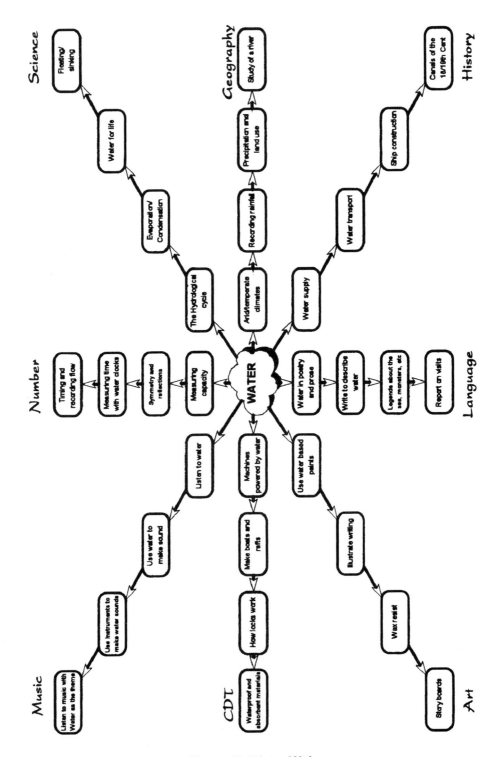

Figure 7: Water Web

Forming Links

When you have a plan which your family are happy with, start to look for links across subject areas. For example, there is a clear link between *Write to describe Water* (Language), *Illustrate writing* (Art) and *Symmetry and Reflections* (Number) on our web. When you have found a link, draw a line on the web to link the boxes, making a spider's web shape.

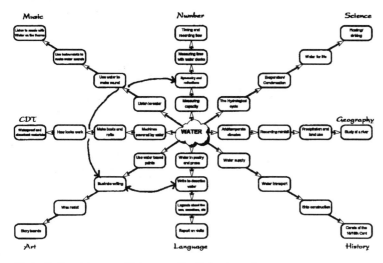

Not all the ideas will be easily linked at first, but in the course of studying one area, questions relating to another completely separate area may arise. This is a joy of home education - one never knows where investigation will lead, or what might be produced as a result.

Teachers sometimes refer to this linking across subject areas as an *Integrated Curriculum*, where studies in different subject areas are related to a central theme. In the days before the National Curriculum it was not uncommon to find this integrated approach or topic work in schools, especially primary schools. Even that was a far more restricted way of learning than is available to the home educator, though. It is unlikely that a class of thirty or more children will work at their own interests in near silence while music is playing in the background. They almost certainly would not be allowed to work on any single activity for as long as they wished - time limits being imposed in school. Neither would they be able to wander from one activity to another, in and out of the classroom, extend their learning through cooking, fixing machinery or take part in real work. Excursions would be arranged and involve worksheets - spontaneity is quashed. Most of all, the opportunities for talking through a concept with another person do not arise. There is more to integrated learning than an integrated curriculum.

"... where's the first boy?"

"Please, Sir, he's cleaning the back parlour window,"...

"So he is, to be sure, "rejoined Squeers. "We go upon the practical mode of teaching, Nickleby; the regular education system. C-l-e-a-n, clean, verb active, to make bright, to scour. W-i-n, win, d-e-r, der, winder , a casement. When a boy knows this out of a book he goes and does it"
Charles Dickens, Nicholas Nickleby

Home education allows learning to occur in all kinds of ways. Effective learning occurs naturally by total involvement in a subject. Imagine a child who is busy making a wax-resist picture of an underwater scene to illustrate a story which he has written and recorded, while in the background a Sea Symphony is playing on a tape. He has made ice lollies which are freezing in the refrigerator, and he has jugs, bottles, tubes and funnels to play with in the bath or paddling pool. Imagine an older sibling who has found out about water in cars, and is now making a detailed drawing of the internal combustion engine. He has mended the sprinkler and adjusted the water to the correct pressure to water the garden, cleaned out the goldfish tank and is thinking about the story he is currently reading while he works at his drawing. How much are they learning? This snapshot is not untypical of many home educators. Effective learning involves all the senses, all of the time.

Having identified a theme and defined a plan of action, you can use it occasionally for reference The learning comes, however, not from making sure that all areas are ticked off but from doing it. Like a shopping list, it is a memory aid, not a prescription. The action of thinking about a single theme in depth, identifying areas of interest and resources, and planning activities around those is often enough. The rest will follow naturally, more so as you and your family become experienced at learning in this way.

 Study becomes meaningful and relevant to everyday life.

> *At lunchtime I went to her front garden. She was sitting there on the lawn, on a spread-out blanket beneath the tree. She had her books, her pencils, her paints scattered around her...*
>
> *She had a book open at a skeleton of a bird. She'd been copying this into her sketch book.*
>
> *"You're doing science?" I said.*
>
> *She laughed.*
>
> *"See how school shutters you,'" she said. "I'm drawing, painting, reading, looking. I'm feeling the sun and the air on my skin. I'm listening to the blackbird's song. I'm opening my mind.'"*
> **David Almond, Skellig**

Providing The Initial Stimulus

If your web has been based upon a child's interest in the first place, it should not be too hard to find some related activity to stimulate learning. In school, the reason for studying any subject is frequently 'because the teacher says so', and the teacher says so because it is on the curriculum/timetable/list of things to be covered before the end of term. At home, learning happens because it is natural and desirable. When an interest has been identified build upon it, by providing more information, if possible in some other form than books. A proactive approach to learning is what schools cannot provide. In fact, they seem to do things the opposite way round! An outing to a place of interest will often provide the climax of a project or study, rather than the reason for finding out more information in the first place. Home educators have far greater opportunity to experience life in the real world and to learn from it than schoolchildren. We can take advantage of those weeks when the majority of children are in school, places of interest are quieter and often entrance fees are cheaper.

First-hand information and experience invariably provides more stimulus for learning than books, as it demands the use of all the senses. Try to find a suitable place to visit, if possible somewhere local to which it would be easy to return at a later date to continue or develop study. Go along for a day out, taking paper, pens, a camera and tape recorder with you if possible. Make sure you pick up as many leaflets and gather as much information as you can.

Action!	Make a list of the places of interest near to your home which might provide some initial stimulus for learning. Mark the ones which you know charge an entrance fee, and those which are free. Where else might you find out about water? Use the telephone directory to find the number of the local water authority, the water treatment plant, the Environment Agency, wildlife or bird sanctuaries etc. Factories and industrial sites sometimes accommodate educational visitors, as do the fire and rescue service, the larger supermarkets and farms, docks, dairies, and swimming pools. Telephone or write to find more resources to visit which will help with developing the topic. What further resources are available? Consider the library, Tourist Information, local newspapers, Internet etc. Commercial enterprises frequently supply useful information; for example the manufacturers of water filters, garden ponds or mineral waters may well have information packs. Particulars of the local rivers may be available from canoeing or angling clubs. Be resourceful!

How To Do It

Developing Learning

> **Action!** Imagine you have taken your family to visit a working water-wheel at a museum. They have watched the wheel, photographed it, put their hand in the water, noticed some fish in the mill pond, talked about what is powering the wheel and looked at the sluice gates. A tape recorder has been used to record the sound of the water-wheel in action. They have bought postcards and a guidebook.
>
> How could you develop the learning which has happened during this visit? How will you do this - by designing some work-sheets, making colouring sheets, using the schools study pack which was on sale at the museum, or by suggesting some other activity? Will you present the 'follow-up work' as something which you expect to be done, or is there another way? Think about how what the children have seen will help them to learn, and how you might develop this at home.

Remember, no-one is going to mark your work. If your spelling and grammar are not too good it really does not matter - it is the ideas which are of importance here. These notes are only for your own reference and will be invaluable when you come to plan other topics in the future.

I hear and I forget.
I see and I remember.
I do and I understand.
Confucius

Using Textbooks

So far the theme of this book has been to emphasise how little home education need or should mirror school's approach to learning. It may come as something of a surprise, then, to find a section on using textbooks. Their place is invaluable, however.

What we become depends on what we read after all of the professors have finished with us. The greatest university of all is a collection of books.
Thomas Carlyle

Clearly, the main objectives of textbooks are as aids to learning. Good textbooks have clear text, functional illustrations and an attractive layout. It may suggest activities to reinforce learning and it might have resources for further research.

Apart from its function as a learning aid, a textbook also empowers the child by giving him the responsibility for his own learning for a while. Such learner-management does not come easily after having school perform this role. On coming out of school children need help in working alone; careful use of textbooks can help with this transition.

Used as a tool for learning, textbooks free the wissian from the immediate responsibility of facilitating learning. Designing and implementing a democratic package of home educating can be extremely demanding. This is natural and to be expected. Many new teachers feel exhausted to the point of having no social life outside of school during the first year of teaching. Even experienced teachers find the job demanding and value their long holidays as a time when they can get back to a normal existence. If you have ever thought of teachers as people who get money for playing in sand and water and then enjoy long holidays, maybe a few weeks of managing home education will change your mind. Using textbooks to supplement learning does give you a break; it also adds structure.

Home educators do not have to use textbooks in the same way as schools, working through the book in a systematic way from beginning to end. Textbooks are particularly useful when they supplement learning which has taken place through experience. For example, you could find references to relevant issues in the topic and use the pages from textbooks when designing a plan of study. The pages about capacity in a maths scheme, river development, the hydrological cycle or wave action in a geography textbook, or a comprehension exercise using text on the theme of 'water' might all fit in with the topic and supplement learning.

The worry about *are they doing enough?* and *are we doing it right?* are common to all new home educators who have taken their children out of school. This may be linked with *is this good enough for the LEA?*, as well as the demands of the children themselves. The children, it seems, often desire a more formal timetable. They like to feel that they are doing 'proper' work. Providing textbooks can have a social advantage, acting rather like a security blanket for parents and children. Perhaps it makes relating to their schooled friends easier.

Our early efforts were very disorganised and chaotic, and it was the children themselves who insisted we create more structure and organisation in their education. One of my most important educational lessons came from this experience, for whilst we adults were assuring our children that any structure to their education was completely unnecessary, and that they could be 'learning all the time', (Holt, 1991), our children were demanding 'timetables'; 'school holidays' and 'proper' work!

Cara Martin, The Holistic Educators

Designing A Plan

When your Topic Web and the accompanying notes are complete they can be used to form the basis of a teaching plan or forecast, something which many LEAs ask to see. A topic like this could provide sufficient work for up to six weeks. It could last even longer. There are no rules. The plan can be used, modified, left for a while and returned to at a later stage. Eventually, one web might link to another - even bigger webs can be made, based on themes.

At this stage you will need to start planning in detail the areas which you intend to study and writing your plans down. You may wish to provide a copy of your plan for the LEA, but do be aware and impress upon the LEA that any plans are open-ended and may change according to the needs and wishes of the learner.

Use the headings from the Teaching Web as a basis for your plan. If you are working with more than one child, you will need to make a set of notes for each child, modified according to the age and ability of each child.

Topic-Based Approach

The scheme is intended to be flexible. Home educators are able to take full advantage of the environment as an aid to learning, and if work must give way to outings either from necessity or for pleasure, the scheme can be picked up again at the next opportunity. This is a structured scheme, however, and it is envisaged that students will work through it on most days in a similar pattern to that followed in schools. As we have already seen, however, home educators do not have the restrictions imposed by the school system.

Frequently, a criticism of home educators is that "they only do reading, writing and arithmetic". The following method of working has been designed to ensure students follow a structured pattern of working with scope for developing other subject areas than the 3 R's while giving sufficient time to basic skills. It encourages practical work and life skills which are so important to home educators, and can be adapted to the needs of the individual.

The scheme of work is based upon each student completing five academic tasks each day. The scheme covers a five-day plan, over which the tasks are rotated. Home educators may prefer to work Monday to Friday, but as they need have no

Plan your work and work your plan
Anon

There are only two lasting bequests we can hope to give to our children. One of these is roots; the other, wings.
Holding Carter

restrictions like weekends or school holidays, they can adjust this to take advantage of using facilities which are often less crowded/expensive during the week, e.g. leisure centres, riding lessons.

The method of organising work described here is structured and detailed. It gives a basic plan, but it is intended to be changed to suit your unique family and its needs. All children are different, and your child will develop interests which he wishes to pursue and for which time should be allocated within the day.

The scheme described is a basic programme which is designed to ensure that:

- where two or more children are being educated together, each gets individual attention,

- a programme of work is tailor-made to suit the child's needs,

- your child has a balanced curriculum, and does more than the 3 R's

- you, the parent, have some time when you can get on with the things which need to be done around the home.

Subject Areas

The study web identified eight subject areas, but when it comes to implementing a package of home education these subject areas need to be further broken down into manageable sections. Language, for instance (not 'English', as it is not always English which is being used!) can be split into reading, writing and reading skills.

Similarly number (not arithmetic or maths, as there is far more to comprehension of number than calculation skills) might involve practical number study, recording and handling data or practice in calculation. By breaking down the subjects into separately identifiable skills-based areas, a balanced scheme can be worked out which will form the basis for the curriculum.

The scheme is based upon each child completing five academic tasks every day on a five day rota. Listed below are the eleven subject areas covered by the scheme with a brief outline of the subject to be studied in each period allocated to it. Some of the subjects have been sub-divided so that there is time for practical work and more formal written tasks. As the activities which you plan from week to week will vary according to the nature of the topic which you are studying the scheme described should be used as a guide to organisation of study times and your approach is expected to be fairly flexible. What is not so flexible is the order in which each of the five tasks is completed each day. This is discussed later.

Reading

Universally acknowledged as the most important skill which can be acquired, this is included every day. Young children should read to an adult every day and even when they become fluent, reading aloud should not be disregarded. In the National Curriculum, reading aloud is a skill which is required and assessed. If home education may be a temporary solution, or if you are still uncertain as to whether or not your child will return to school, this needs to be borne in mind. 'Little and often' is the motto when teaching young children to read. This means your child should read a few pages, or if using a reading scheme, a story every day.

Writing

Any kind of writing is included in this category, e.g. stories, poetry, reports and eye-witness accounts. It also includes any note-making and research which the child may be doing as part of another project. Handwriting is covered in this section.

Reading Skills

This category includes work on grammar, spelling, punctuation and comprehension. For young children, this task might be some pre-reading exercise like matching or working on letter sounds and names. Textbooks and formal exercises are envisaged here for part of the time.

Number

This represents formal work in mathematics, arithmetic, tables etc. - usually in the form of written work. It can involve use of textbooks or maths schemes.

Number Skills

Application of mathematical skills in practical tasks. Any number work which is related to the topic and has a practical basis can be included. It also covers practical skills like weighing, measuring and recording, estimating, money and mental arithmetic - the kind of maths you use every day. Home educators can tie this sort of work in with cooking and cleaning activities around the home, shopping, gardening, looking after pets and so forth. As part of the scheme of work, games which involve counting could be used here, as could sharing activities, problem solving or playing with sand and water.

Art

This covers any kind of art work, depending upon what materials are available at the time. As wide a range of materials as possible for art and craft is desirable and a variety of types, sizes and shapes of paper should be available. Art can usually be tied in with the topic. The opportunities for free expressive art should be numerous, and art materials as freely available as possible, especially when working with young children and/or children who have become disaffected or emotionally disturbed by experiences.

Craft, Design and Technology (CDT)

This means building and making things with a variety of materials and making them work. There are opportunities for this to be linked with project work as well as times for free craft, when children can make whatever they like.

Music

You do not have to be a musician to appreciate music. Make use of the local record library and listen to a variety of music. If you are stuck for a starting point, refer to the project which is currently being studied and find something which you can relate to it. If the child is a musician, this is the time when you have an opportunity for more practice, trying out composition or giving a performance.

Science, Geography And History

With young children my approach to these subjects is usually through the project which is ongoing at any time. Science covers biology, chemistry and physics in the curriculum. Geography includes study of geology and the shape of the land, meteorology and even astronomy, as well as social geography, map-reading and general knowledge of the countries of the world. History links to geography, and the three subjects complement each other well when taken as part of a project. Older children may wish to study any of these subjects in greater depth and extra time may be required for them to do so, perhaps by extending the daily tasks to six periods.

Organising The Rota

The master plan is set out in the table below:

Day	Task 1	2	3	4	5
1	Number	Writing	Art	Reading Skills	Reading
2	Reading	Number Skills	Sc/Geog/His	Writing	Music
3	Writing	Reading Skills	Reading	Number	Art/CDT
4	Reading Skills	Number	Sc/Geog/His	Reading	Music
5	Reading	Number Skills	CDT	Number	Writing

Figure 8: Rota - Master Plan

Read the plan across the chart, so that on Day 1 the child will have the tasks of Number, Writing, Art, Reading Skills and Reading which he will aim to complete. Follow the lines across the master plan for each day's tasks.

Encouraging children to take an active part in decision-making and managing their own education is important if you are working towards an autonomy. At this stage, making each child his own set of activity cards which can be kept or hung in a prominent position and referred to may be considered. For each child you will need five pieces of A5 card - one card for each day on the rota. Each card has the list of activities for each day, as shown. Pre-readers can be given a set of activity cards of their own, and encouraged to read them - this gives an opportunity for reading for information, and a purpose behind the skill of reading.

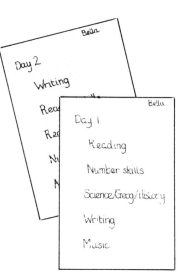

If you are working with more than one child, start each at a different day on the rota, thus ensuring that for the most part, each individual will be working through different activities at different times, and you will have greater opportunity to give each person individual attention. Some activities may clash at times - for instance, we work with four children, so on Day 1 we have two people doing Science/Geog/History at the same slot in the day. Learning can still be personalised, as it may be that for these activities, one child will be working on a different task and in a different subject area form the other. At other times there may well be some benefit in suggesting that two children work together on a practical activity, even if the difference in age range is great. Children often learn best from each other, and co-operative learning situations encourage social awareness and communication skills to develop.

As far as possible it is important to follow the five activities for each day in the order given. Activities in the basic skills which occur late on one day are usually timetabled early the following day, so that the child does not need to miss the most important areas of the curriculum - literacy and numeracy. If the child does not complete the five tasks on any day, there need be no 'finishing off' or extra work on the following day - a factor to be considered when trying to re-establish some self-esteem in a child and to foster a feeling of achievement. The activities have been timetabled to give a balance between written study and practical tasks but generally the whole scheme has a bias towards skills-based learning rather than formal book-learning. You may wish to shift the emphasis to suit the needs of your own children or your personal philosophy.

Designing Learning Plans

This can take the form of notes for your own reference and be done at the beginning of each week. These notes will help to remind you exactly what needs to be covered each week and when you will do each task. Good organisation at this stage will allow you to make the most effective use of your time each day so it is worth giving some thought to your weekly study plans. If you have several children there may be times when they can work together on a task, even if they are of different ages. This is another of the joys of home education; it is one of the reasons why home-educated children are more tolerant of their siblings and learn more effectively than children in school.

A sample sheet of study plans for the first week has been included below. This has been designed with top junior/lower secondary age students in mind and will need to be modified to suit the individual needs of any family.

At first, planning a programme of study takes time. When a system of home education is established and you are working with your children rather than for them, the task of planning will become quicker. The time taken over this stage pays off, however, as more time will be available to spend with your family when the planning and organisation of work is clear.

Study Plan for Week 1

Water Topic

READING BOOKS

Write the names of the books here, of a) those that you hear your child read on a daily basis, b) that the child reads for his interest, and c) any that you may have read to him.

LANGUAGE

Creative Writing

- Start an anthology on the theme of WATER.

- Following a visit or experiment using WATER, write about what you have observed.

Comprehension

Read about the hydrological cycle. Rewrite a description of the process in your own words. Look up the definitions of any words which you do not understand in a dictionary.

Spelling

Learn the following names of seas and oceans. Find out what the names mean, or where they came from:

 Atlantic, Pacific, Arctic, Mediterranean, Indian, China, Sargasso, Caribbean, Baltic

Use an atlas to find out where they are.

NUMBER

Number skills

- Learn 7X table. Find out about the Seven Seas. Find out about the River Severn!

- Start work on Capacity. Introduce a standard measure - pint or litre. Use different shaped containers to measure.

- Introduce fractions of the standard measure - ½, ¼, ¾. Relate to millilitres.

Number

Convert decimal to fractions, fractions to decimals. Find reference and exercises in textbook.

SCIENCE

- Set up a rain gauge, observe the precipitation and record rainfall.

- Study the hydrological cycle. Write to explain what happens and illustrate your work with a diagram. (Link to Language)

- Cooking - observe boiling, freezing, steam, condensation and evaporation. Talk about these changes which occur in water.

GEOGRAPHY

- Observe and identify cloud formations.

- Watch the weather forecasts on T.V. and record them in note form. Compare the forecast with the weather experienced in your area. How many times was the forecast correct?

- Collect weather maps from national newspapers and put them in order in a scrapbook. Look for patterns in the weather which develops over the week. Talk about this.

- Look at rainfall charts in an Atlas, and discuss different climates and rainfall patterns.

HISTORY

- Look for local place names which give a clue to the availability of water - e.g. Coleford. Drybrook, Puddlebrook.

- Find names of large towns which relate to the presence of water - e.g. Bournemouth, Newport, Romford, Eastbourne.

- Find out about the availability of water in your area - are there any water troughs, drinking fountains, wells, pumps, springs, etc. Look for clues to history in the immediate environment.

- Has your town ever experienced flooding? Are any buildings marked with the level which flood water reached? When did the flood occur? Find out more about local history by looking in local museums and local studies sections of the library.

ART

- Experiment with water based paints and different techniques, e.g. drop and puff painting, spatter painting, blotting.

MUSIC

- Listen to the music of the Sorcerer's Apprentice. Read or listen to the story. How has the composer used the instruments to make the sound of water being poured?

CDT

- Use the library to find out about the designs of water-powered machines. Design and make a water-powered machine. See "How Science Works" in Resources.

Working Through The Scheme

You will need:-

- Lots of plain A4 paper and some kind of folder to keep any written work that is produced.

- A copy of your Master Plan, as described above.

- Paper, textbooks, materials etc. to support the study which you have planned.

- A system of rewards if used, for instance, a packet of shiny sticky stars or smiley face rubber stamp.

The Evening Before You Start

You have decided what your project is to be - for the sake of this book we will work on a WATER project. You have settled on a maths scheme which you intend to follow, supplemented by basic number skills books on multiplication tables and basic maths. You have a selection of reading books and story books, perhaps some of a reading scheme, and you know which of the schools television programmes you are going to follow. Art materials are available, as are collections of packaging, tins, empty cartons etc. for CDT and you have some science equipment which you have found in your kitchen cupboards.

Take one sheet of the ruled A4 paper from your folder and copy out Day 1 of the Master Plan, putting the child's name in the space on the left hand side.

Now in a different colour, write exactly what will be done under each task heading and put a big asterisk (*) in the boxes where you will be working with the child. If you have a young child, you will be putting an asterisk in the Reading box, because you will be hearing him read - aim to hear a child learning to read every day. In some of the boxes, the asterisk may mean that you intend to work closely with the child all through the task. In others, it may mean that you intend to start him off on an exercise and leave him to get on with it on his own. You should NOT have an asterisk in every box!

In the space underneath the plan, write down anything which you have to do that day, any household chores which will have to be done, and any notes you may have regarding who cooks dinner. We have already seen how even very small children can help with housework, and should be encouraged to do so.

Our daily plan sheets probably look something like this:-

NAME	TASK 1	2	3	4	5
Adam	Number Capacity P16	Writing* At the sea - poem following visit to beach	Art To illustrate poem	Reading Skills Spellings - 'ea' words - sea, beach, stream etc.	Reading Free reading
Bella	Reading* Level 8 Bk. 6	Number Skills Measuring capacity P 12	Sc/Geog/Hist* Mapwork - OS 1:50,000 sheet - coastline	Writing* Following trip to beach	Music Listening to Sea Interludes, B. Britten
Charlie	Writing* Wet and dry - writing about shells/stones collected at the beach	Reading skills Spellings - 's' initial consonant sound - sea, sand, stream,	Reading* Level 5 bk. 3	Number N.8 2.2 Addition	Art/CDT Painting picture of the seaside
Daisy	Reading Skills initial 's' sound	Number Addition N7 practical	Sc/Geog/Hist* Maps with Bella	Reading* Level 3 Bk. 2	Music as Bella

'Look & Read' BBC2 11.00

Adam - clean bathroom, shopping

Bella - vacuum sitting room, make apple pie

Charlie - sweep down stairs, make fisherman's pie

Daisy - washing-up breakfast, sandwiches for lunch

Pick up prescription from doctor. 'Phone Mum this afternoon. Cubs 6.00 p.m.

Figure 9: Daily Plan Sheet

Be sure that you have all the equipment and materials necessary for the day's work to be completed. Relax before your big day tomorrow.

Next Morning

After breakfast has been cleared away, the child has made his bed, washed etc. have a discussion. Explain that you are aiming to achieve these five things by the end of the day and in this order. Also explain the list of extra activities. If you have more than one child decide on individual tasks, making a note of names beside the jobs on your list as you go.

It may be more practical for the child to get on with household chores at once, while you are organising paper and pens. Aim to settle down to work by about mid-morning. Any cooking which requires your supervision may have to wait until later. We find that making the dinner for early evening does not get done until the afternoon when we can devote some time to whichever children are helping in the kitchen.

When you have agreed what is to happen, in what order, and who is responsible (including yourself) say the magic word GO and see what happens. Set the child off on his study when he is ready and if you are not working with a child, you can get on with the things that you yourself need to do around the house.

Do not be afraid to take a break if and when necessary, but try to encourage your child to get through a fair amount of the tasks before giving up. See the child's work and check it as you go along, i.e. as the child finishes each task (see page 193). At first give lots of praise and encouragement and be generous with the rewards, especially if your child has not been accustomed to praise at school. Display art as soon as possible and encourage praise from others of the family, friends, neighbours etc.

At home, children are spared the frustrations consequent on an inability to understand or failure to produce acceptable pieces of work. Instead they come to see learning as a continuous process. Obstacles to learning are dealt with there and then, or shelved till another time, without loss of face.

Young children cannot be expected to study at this level for much more than an hour or so in total and will need frequent breaks for play and refreshments between tasks. Even older children will find it hard to study intensively for a long time. The five tasks should be completed easily in about two and a half hours total by a child of about ten and perhaps three or three and a half hours by a child of secondary school age.

There are no ticks or crosses. I'm watching all the time. If there's a mistake I tell them straight away. If you mark it later they don't remember... [He] had a lot of difficulty with basic writing. He wrote letters back to front. I've almost cured it by constantly drawing his attention to it. But its got to be done straight away.
Alan Thomas, Educating Children At Home

This may not seem to be very long when compared to the five hours which children spend in school, but home educators can and should take a very different approach from school. At home, we aim to finish five daily tasks by about 2.30 p.m. which allows us time to go shopping and start preparing the evening meal with whichever child who is to help with cooking. Of course, active participation in all of these tasks is a valuable contribution to the whole education process and should not be dismissed. Home education is an ongoing, seamless process and it is therefore impossible to measure how long is spent on it each day, or for how many days of the year. Education in our home goes on for every waking hour, 365 days a year - a good deal more 'full-time' than that offered by school timetables!

At The End Of The Day

Choose a quiet time to take stock of what you have achieved and make a few comments in note form on the back of the first day's sheet. Use your experience to help in future planning. You may wish to make some adjustments to the way you are working or to change a child's work if it is not pitched at the correct level. Be critical, but remember to note down the things which worked well and allow yourself some praise for having survived the first day!

Try to continue the scheme for at least ten days - two five-day weeks - before having a bigger assessment of the way it is working. If it is not working for either yourself or your child, try to identify and discuss the problem areas, and work out how these can be overcome.

At first, a child who is accustomed to the spoon-fed curriculum of school may request a lot of support when working through the day plans, but as the pattern of working becomes established and confidence builds, the learner is able to take greater responsibility for managing his own learning pattern and organising the time he spends upon each activity. Older learners may wish to drop some of the activities like reading skills which are more relevant to younger children, and to replace them with more activities which are more appropriate to their specific needs, the study of a specialist skill or language, perhaps. Sometimes it is appropriate to add another activity to the day plan, if a child is studying for an examination, for example, and the plan should be adapted to accommodate this. We have found that there are times when a 'free day' or 'finishing-off day' is called for, when any child can choose to abandon the plan and take time out to complete a

In school, children spend only two-thirds of their time on task. It does not follow that they are actively learning when they are on task, only that they are doing something which in interpreted as productive. How much of that time is actually spent actively learning is unknown, In addition, work is often not matched to the ability of the child (Bennett et al. 1984). At home, on the other hand, children spend most of their time at the frontiers of their learning. Their parents are fully aware of what they already know and of the next step to be learned. Learning is therefore more demanding and intensive.
Alan Thomas, Educating Children At Home

part of a project or a particular study. The plan can and should be picked up and put down, according to the dictates of time and opportunity for learning. There is little value in home education if it becomes as school, operating to the exclusion of every other part of life. Home educators are free to seize the opportunity of the moment, and although the plan is useful in defining the organisation of productive learning time at home, it is not the be-all-and-end-all of home education.

We should like to stress that this plan is a suggestion of a way to proceed with home education. Researchers have observed how home educators appear to vary between structured and informal systems as confidence improves; this may also be the result of particular demands of the children and their needs,

Chapter Eight

Academic Subjects

"Reeling and Writhing, of course, to begin with," the Mock Turtle replied; "and then the different branches of Arithmetic - Ambition, Distraction, Uglification, and Derision."

Lewis Carroll, Alice's Adventures In Wonderland

General

This chapter gives a general overview of the way in which each of the separate subject areas familiar in the school curriculum may be approached by home educators. Each area represents a body of knowledge which is important in its own right, but to enable children to learn in a multisensory environment some links must be forged across the various subject areas and further. As we have seen, planning a scheme of study around a central theme and identifying links across the subjects to form a study web is one way in which multisensory learning can be at least partially achieved. The home educator is in a unique position of being able to extend the opportunities for learning to embrace all of life's experiences, making full use of the environment of the home and the extended environment on a local, national or even global scale. No other learning system is able to offer this holistic basis through which multisensory and meaningful learning can occur naturally and autonomously.

In this chapter we give some general advice on teaching and learning which home educating parents may find helpful. It would not be appropriate in this book to give a great amount of information on the current thinking behind the teaching of each subject, or to discuss in detail the remedial actions which can or should be taken when learning fails to progress at the expected rate. There are many good specialist books available now which can be referred to. We have listed some which we have found most useful, readable and easy to understand in the bibliography.

Teaching Your Child To Read

The ability to read is acknowledged as the most important skill which children are taught in school. Reading and literacy skills have a high profile at the moment, fuelled by the introduction of the Literacy Hour in state schools, the National Year of Reading (1999) and the continuing quest to raise standards in education by initiatives such as homework clubs and holiday learning schemes.

A tremendous amount has been written about the teaching of reading, the different approaches which can be used, and the teaching methods which should or should not be employed. Everywhere fashions come and go and the world of education is no exception. In the 1960s the teaching of phonics (the way the letters of the alphabet sound) went out of vogue, and children were encouraged to recognise words by the shape they made on the page. Reading schemes fell from favour, and teachers banned them from the classroom in favour of 'real' books. For twenty years reading round the class, or group reading has been banished. Now it seems to be making a comeback, alongside spelling tests and traditional phonics - The Initial Teaching Alphabet of the late sixties as a fast-track method of teaching reading has gone, but in its place schools use schemes like THRASS. Even *Janet And John* is being revamped. Back come Enid Blyton's *Famous Five* and *Noddy*. Schools are once again buying sets of books for group reading lessons. 'Big Books' - large versions of familiar children's books - have been produced specifically to support the Literacy Hour and are used extensively in schools. Teachers are now being instructed how to use these big books with a whole class, by pointing at each word with a stick. Is this a return to Victorian classroom methods? Whatever the justification for such an approach, it seems unlikely that a love of books and an appreciation of literature will result.

Home educators are not under pressure to teach children to read at an early age. Nor need they succumb to attainment targets, testing or assessment. They can allow reading to develop naturally and at the child's pace rather than that dictated by the Government. As the preoccupation with standards of literacy continues, evidence that early reading may actually be damaging or at least undesirable is coming to light. Media coverage and documentaries presenting evidence against the early teaching of reading in our schools in the UK has caused parents to question the methods being used to get children reading early. For many years, this has been a questionable practice. In Europe, formal education does not begin until children are seven years old; followers of Rudolph

Steiner's philosophy discourage children from learning to read until they have reached the age of seven. A comment upon the later teaching of reading is that the general standard of adult literacy is no less in countries where reading is not formally taught until children are seven years old.

An interesting observation of home-educated children is that they tend to learn to read at a later age than their peer group in school, but they appear to become fluent readers much more quickly. Researchers have also noted that both boys and girls tend to be avid readers, although the evidence from schools is that boys in particular seem to lose interest in reading, particularly when they reach the top end of the primary/lower secondary school.

Preparing To Teach Your Child To Read

A love of language and recognition of rhythm in sounds are the first steps towards developing fluency in reading. Articles about reading development often suggest that this can begin at a very early age, by parents sharing story books with babies as soon as the child is able to focus on the page - about three months old. Maybe it starts earlier, even before birth, as babies in the womb hear and respond to sounds outside, especially the sound of their parents' and siblings' voices and familiar music.

Young babies enjoy colours, patterns and movement. As they grow they are able to distinguish shapes and to relate pictures to experiences in the real world. There is no need for any formal teaching to take place with very young children. Sharing books and talking with a child about the pictures is enough to instil the initial enthusiasm for learning. It may be stating the obvious, but for anyone to want to read they have to believe that it is a pleasant, desirable and natural experience. In this respect, reading should never become a chore.

Sequencing and learning by rote are important pre-reading skills. Can your child recite the days of the week? Does he know the names of the colours? Can he count to ten, forwards and backwards? Can he match pictures, complete simple patterns and sequences, thread beads in order, match shapes and sizes, and know about spatial concepts like above and below, under and over, taller and smaller? All these things may seem too simple to be worth mentioning but they are very important pre-reading skills, and reception teachers spend a lot of time teaching these concepts to children before they are ready to read.

> *...a good measure of the parents' success in teaching reading, is that home-educated children generally become enthusiastic, often insatiable readers. Most surprising, and intriguing, is that a significant number of children do not learn to read until very late, between 8 and 10 years of age, apparently without detriment.*
> **Alan Thomas, Educating Children At Home**

Identifying Learning Difficulties

Inability or difficulty with performing these skills may indicate dyspraxia or dyslexia, although proper diagnosis of these conditions requires the specialist knowledge of an Educational Psychologist or a dyslexia specialist. Parents should not be unduly alarmed if sequencing does not come easily to their children. Should a child still have difficulty with counting, reciting the days of the week, writes numbers or letters backwards or finds following from left to right unnatural and uncomfortable after he is seven or eight, and his ability to read is a cause for concern, it may be the time to contact a specialist for an informal assessment and professional advice. A specialist teacher will be able to diagnose the level of learning difficulty, suggest reasons and remedial action which can be taken. Often an eye test by a qualified ophthalmic optician will identify a visual problem which can be easily overcome. Sometimes it is purposeful activity which will spur a child on - a child who makes mistakes in counting out bricks for a number exercise may make far fewer mistakes when counting out the same number of sweets into a bag.

It must be mentioned at this point that many dyslexics are also 'gifted' people - a phenomenon which can be the root cause of disruptive behaviour in school (or at home) when a child with a very high IQ is bored. There are specialist organisations and support groups which will give help to families with dyslexics and gifted dyslexics.

Many dyslexics are left-handed, but not all. Left-handedness should not be taken as an early indication of dyslexia. Children may not make up their minds which hand to write with until they are about seven, and it is a serious mistake to attempt to force a young child to use his right hand when using a pencil.

Children will write letters and numbers backwards. This is quite natural and nothing to worry about, unless it happens frequently and the child remains unable to see his mistake. Home educators are able to work alongside their children and correct backward writing immediately. Before jumping to the conclusion that you have a dyslexic in the family on the grounds that letters and numbers are written backwards, try this "magic" trick: when your child next writes a letter or number backwards, point out his mistake by trying to get him to see what is wrong. When he has identified that the shape is backwards, ask the child to turn with his back to you, and with your finger, write the offending number correctly on his back, saying the letter or number as you do it. Do this three times, then ask the child to go and write the letter/number again on a piece of paper. Very frequently this simple corrective technique works; it may not be a total cure, but it effects a vast improvement.

The diagnosis of dyspraxia (Clumsy Child Syndrome), dyslexia or dyscalculia (the number form of dyslexia) is the job of a professional Educational Psychologist or qualified specialist, and should not be attempted by a non-specialist parent or teacher. There are, however, a few clues which may be helpful to the parent or lay-person in identification of specific learning difficulties in children. If you have a child who is having difficulty with reading after the time when they have "changed their teeth" the following check list might be of help:

- Crawling seems to indicate a stage of development which many dyslexic children miss. Did your child pass by the crawling stage?

- Most children start to walk at about their first birthday. Did your child start to walk very early or late?

- Does your child seem to need to see something happening in number to understand it? For example, can he add and take away when given real situations, but find the same task difficult when asked to do a sum in his head?

- Does your child have problems with the concept of time? Is he often unaware of time, frequently late or up very early, unable to be hurried? Does he find waiting difficult?

- Does your child appear to have difficulty sequencing letters in the alphabet, numbers on a number line, days of the week, months of the year, etc.? When he dresses himself, does he put on his clothes in the wrong order?

- Ask your child to draw a picture of a person. Afterwards, study the picture. Look for the amount of detail shown - hair, fingers on hands, facial features, clothes. Look at the various parts of the body and how they are joined. Check whether the person is standing on the ground. Is the drawing rather immature or lacking in detail which you might have expected?

- Ask your child to read, or look at a book with him. Watch his eye movements. Do his eyes appear to dart about the page, searching for clues from the pictures? Does he read words back to front (reading 'saw' for 'was') or even upside-down?

- Does he ever complain of numbers or letters 'moving' or 'dancing' on the page, especially when a piece of printed text is giving problems?

- Does he have difficulty throwing, catching or kicking a ball? Does skipping, hopping or clapping in time to music seem hard to him?

- Usually a child will be able to stand on one foot whilst reciting a well-known nursery rhyme, or singing a simple familiar song. Is this difficult for him?

This is NOT a diagnostic test for dyslexia. If, however, your seven- or eight-year-old is having difficulty reading and you have answered *yes* to some or all of the questions with little hesitation, it may be time to seek specialist help. Begin by making an appointment for an eye test. Ask the GP if the child can have his hearing checked, and contact one of the dyslexia support groups to find out about having an informal assessment performed. This may need to be paid for, but the cost should be nowhere near that of a formal diagnosis, which may run to over £200 for the consultancy fee of an Educational Psychologist. A list of help groups is given at the end of this book.

Providing Books

Always provide plenty of books for your child. Show from the outset that books are things of value and not to be left out in the garden or on the floor, and never to be scribbled in or drawn on. Before reading can take place a child has to want to read. Making books available and attractive is paramount to motivating reading, so storing books in a place which is inaccessible to your child is not going to help him learn to read.

When buying books, remember that they are presented so that they are attractive to the parents, who have the money. There are some highly-respected books that do not interest children nearly as much as their parents would like to think.

Storage can present a problem. Some books are too big to fit easily onto the shelf, some are too small to stack comfortably and many are thin volumes which become lost if stored on conventional shelves with spine outwards. Book shops and libraries often use display racks where books are stored flat and the cover shows, but at home this is often impossible where space is usually at a premium. We find that large coloured plastic storage boxes, however, hold a lot of books of all shapes and sizes, and they can be easily flicked though and found when required.

Although books are expensive there are ways in which the cost of providing books can be eased. There are plenty of good book clubs which specialise in children's literature and advertise regularly through the post or in parenting magazines. Some book shops will give a discount on books for home educators. Ask if discount is available when you buy books, and produce some kind of identification as a home educator to back your claim, e.g. a membership card from a recognised home education support group. Look out for discount book shops and sales, and make full use of your local library.

Many libraries have sales of old books. Although these are no longer viable for the kind of use they get in a library they are often very suitable for a family to own. Be wary, however, of buying tatty books; the content may still be good, but if a book looks unattractive a child is unlikely to pick it up and read it for pleasure.

Set An Example

How important is reading to you, the parents? Studies of the reading ability of children have shown that children from homes where books are always in evidence and parents read regularly progress much faster in reading than children from homes where there are no books and the parents do not read.

Action! Do your children see you reading for pleasure and information? Do you have a daily newspaper? Do you use cookery books and enjoy magazines? Are books used and read often? Are books freely available to all members of the family? Are you a member of the library or a book club?

Your actions as a parent give a message to your children. If books are not evident in your home, if you are seldom seen reading or writing, the message given is that this activity is not very important. The availability of books at all levels of reading ability is important, from children's books to encyclopaedias, magazines to reference books and manuals. The first step towards success in the teaching of reading is to ensure that reading is an enjoyable, desirable activity. Children who grow up surrounded by books and seeing adults using books for information and pleasure will grow with the understanding and expectation that reading is a normal and desirable part of adult life.

A Word Of Warning

Not all books may be suitable for children, what you make available is at your discretion. Be aware, however, that if the LEA visit they will make at least a mental note of the reading material to which the child has access and, whether or not you agree with their visit, part of their brief is to be aware of any signs of child abuse. It may not be a direct sign of abuse at all, but it is alarming for a teacher to have an eight-year-old bring *The Joy of Sex* into school to show the class. As a home educator you are being watched by neighbours, friends, relatives, total strangers (library assistants, for instance), the LEA, Health Visitors, GPs, etc. and you are accountable for what your child receives in the way of education.

Learning To Read

📖 *The child recognises that the book holds a story*

By reading to your child from an early age, he will learn to associate stories and information with written text. He will watch you turn pages and so learn the mechanics of a book. He will learn stories by heart - and will probably object if you deviate from the words he remembers - and he will grow to follow stories with the accompanying pictures. Memorising and sequencing are recognised as being among the initial steps in learning to read, so reading to, playing and talking with your child are important.

📖 *The funny squiggles are words*

At first the pictures in books are what the child relates to. The funny squiggles at the top or bottom of the page have no significance to a young baby. It is only with time that a child comes to realise that these squiggles are related to the words which you, the parent, are saying every time you read the book together. A small child will learn a book off by heart from hearing it read time and again. You may well see a child 'reading' a familiar story to himself, turning the pages of a book and reciting the text on each page. He is not reading, but he is treading the first steps down that way.

The realisation that the written word means something is significant in learning to read. Before long children become aware of how much text there is about them, on road signs, packaging, the television, the computer and of course, in books, newspapers and magazines. The greater the child's exposure to the written word, the greater their desire will be to read, and through reading to have access to a world which has so far been closed to them.

They probably see you writing, too. Mummy makes those funny squiggles on a piece of paper with a pen, and treats the paper as if it were important. You may write a shopping list, a letter, or jot down a message from a telephone call. These squiggles are evidently important grow-up ways of communicating, and a young child will naturally be curious and start to copy your actions. He is ready to read.

Reading is a complex skill, requiring far more than the ability to learn the alphabet, or the names and sounds of each letter. These are important, but are used as tools, contributing to the clues both within the context of the text, within any illustrations and from prior knowledge and experience, all of which at some point are used to enable reading.

📖 The child learns individual letters

The ability to identify individual letters is clearly linked to pattern recognition, but in relation to reading the written word it can be hard. Consider that g, g, g, G and G are all the same letter - do they look the same and can they be recognised as such? Is your child able to read your handwriting?

Some people write for children by printing in Capital letters, considering that this will make it easier for the child to read. In fact, as children tend to learn to read in the initial stages as much by recognising the shape of words, printing in capital letters can make reading more difficult! For example, the printed word "flower" is clearly a different shape from the word "cat". When accompanied by the appropriate illustration, as in a child's picture book, the child learns to read by using the clues presented, combined with recognition of the shape made by the letters.

How do you write for your child? As well as being aware of the shape of words yourself, if possible encourage friends and relatives to write in normal, clear handwriting when writing to children, using capital and lower case letters as appropriate.

There are lots of attractive alphabet books which will help children to learn to recognise individual letter shapes and associate the letters with the initial sounds of words: A is for Apple etc. These should not be too heavily relied upon, however. A is for Apple, but it is also for Acorn, and there is a clear difference in the sound made by the letter (grapheme) A.

Many schools use Letterland as a scheme for teaching the child the shapes and sounds of the letters. If your child has experienced Letterland at a playgroup, nursery or in school they have probably enjoyed seeing and recognising Clever Cat, Poor Peter and the Wicked Water Witch long before real reading starts. Such schemes are child-friendly and have much to commend them, but they are not without drawbacks. Children can become so engrossed in Letterland characters and stories that they lose sight of the real sounds of the letters. The process of learning to read can be hampered rather than helped by too much of any scheme used in isolation.

📖 The child recognises his own name

Learning to recognise the shapes and sounds of individual letters is an important step in learning to read, but the first attempts at reading are often through recognition of the shapes of whole words, rather than the building of words using the sound of individual letters. The child will see the letters spelling his own name and associate it with the name itself. It is not the sound of each individual letter or the combination of letters in groups that he associates with at this stage, but the shape of the word. Learning to read by recognising the shapes of words in this way is known as the *look and say* method.

Be careful, though. Infant teachers who gave each new child in the class a necklace with their name clearly printed on it found that all the children soon recognised and even wrote their own names beautifully - upside down!

At this stage the pre-reading games really begin to be applied. Young William will match the first letter of his name to the label on the Weetabix packet, and joyously claim it as his own. Encourage this matching game. Point out labels and associate them with the initial sounds of the words on such things as food packages when you go shopping. Daisy is able to distinguish Double cream from Single, is delighted to read *Dates, Doughnuts* and *Dog Food*, and examines the mail closely for any sign of her initial on the envelope. Point out that the first sound in the new word starts with the same sound and the same letter as the familiar letter at the start of the child's name. Gradually, by working in this way and keeping sessions frequent and low-key, your child will become familiar with the sound and shape of each letter and combination of letters (digraph).

You may start with initial sounds. When these are really familiar, move on to final sounds - *extra s* making a plural, a final *y* making an *ee* sound as in Daisy, Mary etc. and final digraphs like *er* in Mother, Father, sister, brother.

At the same time, introduce simple reading books or a reading scheme. Take about ten minutes each day to sit with your child and his book, talk about it, read it to him and hear him read it.

Familiarity with the sounds made by each letter help children to build the skills of what teachers call 'word attack'. The sounds of letters are the tools we use to work out what unfamiliar words say - the skills of *sounding* or working out a new word. This is *phonics*.

English is such a strange language, derived from a mixture of many other languages, and with curious illogical spellings and pronunciations that it is not always possible to read words using phonic skills in isolation. Sometimes unfamiliar words can be found from reading the clues in the context of the text - reading up to and after the unfamiliar word and looking for initial and final sounds within the word can help young readers to make an educated guess at a word they do not know (the BBC programme *Look And Read* presents this strategy well with the 'Blurry Word' Game).

Sometimes the shape made by the letters on the page combined with prior experience of the word are enough to jog the memory of the reader - we know, for instance, that *tion* in a word says *shun*, or that *gh* says *f,* as in cough, because of experience as readers. The process of learning to read is clearly complex and involves many skills of strategy and memory. Once, after a child at a school had at last achieved the ability to read, the infant teacher (who was nearing retirement) remarked, "...after all these years of teaching children to read, I still don't know how they do it. How children learn to read is a mystery to me!"

What is clear is that, as with so much in teaching and learning, *little and often* seems to be the key when one is deliberately trying to give a child a new skill. A little practice at frequent intervals is generally a far more effective strategy for learning than an intensive period of learning. Few people can say, for example, "Today I am going to learn to play the piano", and, having never touched a keyboard before, be able to play confidently through a Beethoven Sonata by bedtime. So it is with reading. Children in school are taught to read, and expected to be able to do so to a measurable standard by the age of seven, by being given frequent opportunities for practice and a structured reading scheme. Children at home can learn to read in the same way if this is considered desirable. Home-educated children do not have to conform to the national standards as set in schools, but it should be acknowledged that many young children want to learn to read and enjoy the individual attention of a parent hearing them read. If you are not certain about your long-term commitment to home education, or whether your child will return to school in the future, it may be unfair on the child to deprive him of learning to read at the same time as his peer group in school, as this would naturally set him at a disadvantage if and when he goes to school and needs to cope with written text.

Hearing Children Read

If you are proactive in teaching a child to read, hearing reading is a discipline - it should develop to the level of a habit, something to be done every day like cleaning teeth, making the bed, putting the milk bottles out...! Hearing reading need take only a matter of ten minutes, but to be effective it needs to be done regularly and become a natural way of life until the child is confident and capable of reading on his own.

Combined with this discipline, reading must be enjoyable for the child - an activity to be keenly anticipated, not dreaded or seen as a chore. The aim is to instil a love of literature and a desire to read. The emphasis in schools has been to hear as many children as possible read every day.

Quite alarmingly, we have come across cases where the teacher will call the morning register while children are reading out from their books. In this way, two more ticks can be added to the teacher's chart of children to be heard. The children, however, are unlikely to have received the message that their skills are appreciated or that the reading material is of any importance.

How To Hear A Child Read

Establish a rule - possibly the only unbreakable rule which is ever imposed:

Nobody interrupts while we are reading; everything else waits

Once the rule is established and understood it can work with everyone except babies and toddlers, for whom, of course, rules do not apply. If you have a baby in the house, reading will need to be put off until a time when the baby is quiet or the toddler occupied; it is most important that reading time is a period which is entirely devoted to the needs of the learner and, as nearly as possible, completely without distraction.

Find a comfortable place to sit and hear the child read. At home, the sofa or at the table is suitable. Make sure the area is well lit and that the child has the book straight in front of him. Teachers become expert at reading and writing sideways or upside-down after years of practice. Holding the book up in front of the child's face is not helpful to either learner or teacher. Have the book on a flat surface or in a position where both of you can see the text. Be ready to help by pointing to a word or sentence, or by obscuring part of the text with a finger or card - a bookmark is an ideal tool for this.

Before beginning to hear a child read, talk about the book - what does the front cover show? What is the title of the book? Read it, and point it out to the child. Open the book to the title page, and read the title again with the child. Turn to the first page, and encourage the child to make some comment or observation about the illustrations before starting to read. This may take only a few minutes, but it is valuable background feeling for the book which is about to be read, and serves as a method of recapping on the characters in a reading scheme, or reinforcing knowledge of words which have already been encountered. By talking about books children learn to appreciate and criticise stories, and to look critically and thoughtfully at illustrations to the text.

As the child reads, encourage the left-to-right movement along the text. Young children often have some difficulty doing this for long. Their eye movements jump forwards and back along the line of print, and sometimes up or down to lines above or below the line which is being read. Using a card or bookmark under the line which is being read can help with this problem, or covering words in the line and uncovering them from the right as the child reads them can help children who find moving from left to right along the lines difficult. Most children go through this stage of jumping about on the text, and usually the parent need not be alarmed. If the problem continues, however, and a child fails to make steady progress in reading it may be worth getting an eyesight test or consulting an experienced professional advisor in reading.

Children who are enjoying a book or making sense of a story will naturally take time to look at the illustrations, and they should be allowed to do this in an unhurried way. There is a difference in reading between 'barking at print', i.e. the ability to sound out and read words on the page without paying any attention to the meaning of the words, and reading for pleasure and understanding. It is the latter which we wish to nurture in young readers. Home educators are in the position of being able to give more time and attention to doing this on an individual basis than schools, and should use this time to their advantage.

As reading ability develops, the grammar and punctuation can be pointed out and discussed as the subject arises. For example, when the child runs two sentences together, the wissian might stop the child an point out the full-stop and capital letter, and re-read the sentence to the child emphasising the pause indicated by the punctuation marks. At this stage it is sometimes useful to re-read a few sentences to a child, putting in expression and emphasising punctuation to bring the story to life.

When a book is finished, the child should be encouraged to find another book which he can read next. If you are using a reading scheme or have organised the reading books into some kind of system whereby they are graded according to difficulty, this should be easy enough for each child to do. The advantage of allowing the child to choose a book to read is that he will be able to find one which is attractive and motivating to him, even if it does not necessarily follow on in the exact sequence.

Keeping A Record

Give the child a bookmark. A piece of stiff paper or card about 5x12 cm should be fine. This will serve as a bookmark and a reading record. Write the child's name on the top, the title or number of the book they are reading, the date and the page number they have reached. If more than one adult is able to hear them read, you may wish to put your initials on the card when you have heard the child read as a record of who has heard the child and when. The card can also be used to write any comments - Well done!, and keep any record of rewards, e.g. stars, smiley faces. When the bookmark is full transfer the information to a more permanent record book.

Shared/Paired Reading

This strategy can work well and be most enjoyable when used in a parent/child context. The idea is that a longer story can be read and shared between the two people. Before you begin, agree on some non-verbal sign which you both understand means "you read now", it might be that the reader touches the listener on the arm, or knocks on the table for instance, when he wants the other person to take over the reading. One reads while the other listens and follows the text. When the first has read enough, he makes the sign and the other reader takes over for a while.

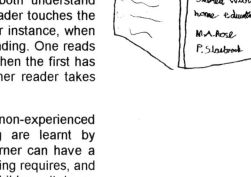

Working in this way with an experienced and non-experienced reader, the skills of expression in reading are learnt by example rather than direct teaching. The learner can have a rest from the intense concentration which reading requires, and a story can be shared and enjoyed. For children, it is an opportunity to read a book which might be a little too difficult for them to read on their own, their vocabulary will extend as they pick up the meaning of unfamiliar words from the context and at the same time, see the word in print. Shared/paired reading has proved to be a successful method of learning to read, and it seems to be particularly useful when children have begun reading but are still not fluent readers - when the stage has been reached where they want to read *The Famous Five* but cannot manage all the words or comprehend the story by themselves.

Reading Schemes v. Real Reading Books

The term *Reading Scheme* refers to the sets of books which are schools use to teach young children to read. These books are carefully designed to be efficient in instructing young children to read through use of a very structured programme. The books are attractive to children of infant school age, with content appropriate to the interests of young children, and of a size which they find easy to handle. The length of the books is also important. The first readers are usually short books, or contain several short stories, so that children can develop a sense of achievement when they read a whole book or a whole story at a time. There are many reading schemes which are used in schools, and some, but not all are available in High Street book sellers. The most frequently used reading schemes include:

- **The Oxford Reading Tree** - Biff and Chip may be familiar characters, and the books are graded by reference to birds - Wrens, Sparrows, etc.

- **Ginn Reading 360** - a variety of stories and poems, the books use many different fonts and styles of writing.

- **Fuzz-Buzz** - often used for remedial teaching

- **1,2,3 and Away** - Billy Blue-Hat, Roger Red-Hat, etc. who live at the Village With Three Corners.

It has to be acknowledged that some of these schemes look extremely dull, both in presentation and in content, but what appears deadly to an adult may be quite attractive to a child. Many children have learnt to read on a diet of 1,2,3 and Away, and seem to accept the books without question, though whether they enjoy reading the books or enjoy the achievement of being able to tick another story about Grandfather Yellow-Hat off the list is questionable. For some children who long to read and have the innate discipline to read a book every day, reading schemes can work well. They give you and the child a measure of success, as the books are carefully graded, and the child moves from one to another in, step by step, book by book. Supplementary readers are available for those times when the learning curve flattens off, and all kinds of support materials to go with the books can be bought from the publishers - rubber stamps depicting characters, worksheets, stickers etc.

It is natural for children learning to read to make rapid progress, then go through periods when they appear to make very little headway at all. At these times there is little point in ploughing on through any particular reading scheme for no better reason than "to teach the child to read". If at all possible, find other books at the same level which can be read by the child until such time as he is ready to move on. Access to as many reading schemes as possible can be an advantage to early readers at such times. Achievement is more important to the learner than progression to the next level.

For two of our children, reading schemes worked well, and they learnt to read at an early age. For one child, however, application to the reading scheme was clearly like training a dog to jump through a hoop. Ben had no interest in the scheme, and although he would read if asked, he had no desire to do so. At the age of seven, he still was not reading although obviously bright, creative and intelligent. At this time he developed a profound interest in Ancient Egypt, and this interest became all consuming. Within weeks Ben had taught

himself to read, not only English, in order to read the many books he had about Ancient Egypt, but he had taught himself hieroglyphics, too!

There are many lovely books for children which are not part of reading schemes. As with anything else, if no pleasure is derived form any activity it is hard to see where the motivation to take part in that activity comes from. Reading schemes work for some and not for others. Once again, learning is a personalised, individual process, and to be successful the teaching methods employed need to be tailor made to fit the learner.

Unfortunately, the subject matter of reading schemes is geared to schoolchildren of the appropriate key stage. The problems are two-fold: the school environment which is featured may well be unfamiliar to a home-educated child, and an older person who has not started reading at the prescribed age is unlikely to be enchanted by such characters as Billy Blue-Hat or Biff and Chip. We would recommend putting pressure on the publishers of reading schemes to include a wider variety of material in this area.

Writing

The skills of writing, although linked with the ability to read, seem to develop naturally after reading. Children realise at an early age that the squiggly signs which adults make on paper with a pen can convey a message, and even as toddlers, children often 'write' and 'read' their messages back. This is known as emergent writing, and for a while it was encouraged in schools, although regrettably it seems to have been abandoned now by some teachers. Encouragement of emergent writing seems to be something which home educators can use to their advantage, however, as it is based upon a natural progression from scribble and pattern forming to this idea of shapes on the page conveying a message. It can happen at the child's pace, making learning truly learner-managed, and it gives the child some reason for writing other than to please the teacher, or because writing is on the timetable.

The basic idea works in this way. A child makes some marks on a piece of paper, draws a picture, perhaps, and presents it to you. Naturally, you praise the child's efforts, and might say:

"What have you drawn a picture of, Eddie?"

"Eddie and Daisy in the paddling pool," comes the reply. "And this is the sun, ... and all the water is coming out!"

"That's lovely. Daisy has got a big smile, hasn't she?"

"Yes."

"And what is this pink, here?" pointing to a large pink blob on one side of the paper.

"That's the flowers. And this is the swing, and this is Eddie!"

"Oh, I see! Well, this is a lovely picture. Can we pin it on the door?"

"Yes"

"Should we put your name on it, so we know that you made this picture?"

"Yes. You write EDDIE."

"Well, can you write EDDIE?"

"Yes"

He takes a pencil and laboriously makes some marks on the paper. Notice that he works from left to right, although his 'writing' tends to go up and down.

"There. EDDIE. Now you pin it on the door, Mummy."

"Okay. Would you like me to write 'Eddie' in book writing underneath your writing?"

"Um. Yes, please."

Eddie watches as I form the letters under his, and say his name again. I point it out to him, moving my finger from left to right along the word, and say, "That says 'Eddie'."

He repeats the actions and 'reads' his name.

Later, I see him repeating the same action again and 'reading' his name on the picture. He shows other members of the family, too, and reads his name again.

Let us go through the conversation above again and pick out some significant points:

i. The child produced a drawing, and through dialogue he gave an explanation of the message in the picture.

Dialogue (speaking, listening and sequencing ideas) comes first

ii. He realised the need for writing - to tell everyone whose picture it was. Knowing that he cannot do real writing (he seems to know this himself. No one has told him that he is lacking this skill) he asks me to write for him. He points to where he wants the writing to be.

Writing has some purpose

iii. I could have written his name for him, and perhaps at an earlier stage, would have done so, but my knowledge of the child is that he understands the concept of writing, and that it is different to drawing, so I ask him to do the job himself.

Don't do something for a child if he can do it himself.

iv. Eddie writes his name and is praised for his attempt. No part of the word was recognisable, but he did work from left to right, and chose to write with a pencil - not use crayon as he had when drawing the picture.

Watch, learn from the child's actions, and build upon their knowledge and understanding.

v. He re-reads his writing to me. Here he is confirming, 'this is what it says'. He understands that writing means something, and that I need to know what it means. He is also proud of the fact that he has 'written' it himself, and his confidence is growing! Perhaps he knows that I cannot read his style of writing?

Listen to the child. What do they know? What are they unsure of? How will you proceed from here?

vi. More praise is accompanied by an offer to help: 'Shall I write it in book writing underneath?' Notice here I used the term *'book writing'* - the sort of writing we see in books, not *proper writing*, or *shall I do it properly*, which would imply criticism of the efforts of the child.

At no time is the child's effort criticised. Only praise is given. The offer to help - which would move the learner forward on the path to reading and writing - can be declined by the learner. He remains in control.

vii. At the child's request, I write the same word underneath his own. Underneath, because the child's writing remains in a more important position on the page, but when the picture is pinned up, the 'book writing' will appear at his eye-level and be more prominent to him, and the child's eye movements will naturally move up and down across the writing, matching his own writing to mine.

Write underneath the child's writing.

But when children copy your writing, they write underneath, so that they do not obscure the words they are copying with their own hand.

Eddie read and re-read his name several times, when he produced the picture and over the following few days when it was pinned on the door. I saw him stop as he passed the door, stop, look and read the writing, sometimes tracing over my writing with his finger, and saying his name. Here is an example of the importance of display of children's work.

The next step towards promoting writing is to continue with pursuing the idea that writing conveys a message from the writer to the reader. Had Eddie brought the picture to me at a later stage in his understanding, my reaction might have been to encourage him to write a sentence about it, using his own words. For example, I might have stopped at the point where he said, "Eddie and Daisy in the paddling pool", and asked him to write that as a title. The procedure from that point would have been the same, however, offering to write in 'book writing', i.e. text which any reader can understand. Sometimes these offers are declined, and that is perfectly acceptable. Maybe the child is satisfied with his own piece of work and does not wish for any outside interference, or perhaps he is simply not ready to have a whole sentence of 'book writing' to cope with.

We tend to work in this way quite a lot when children are learning to write - getting words from the child and either asking the child to write, or writing from the child's dictation to illustrate a creative piece of work like a painting, a drawing or a model. This is the reverse of the school approach which many of us may remember, write, then draw. That way round, the act of writing is given more significance and the drawing is firmly in the place of a time-filler activity or something to illustrate the text.

Naturally, the first means of conveying a message which human beings use is art. Cave dwellers drew cartoon-like pictures on their walls, the creators of the Bayeux Tapestry used pictures to record the events leading up to the Norman invasion and William's conquest at Hastings in 1066. Stained glass windows depict scenes from Biblical stories...of course, few people were literate until relatively recently, but pictorial representation remains important in conveying messages even now. Art and graphic design is a powerful and primary tool in conveying messages. The written word can be used to support those messages, as much as the illustrations being used to support the text, as in this book. It is a sad reflection upon school culture that at the end of the second millennium so little value is attributed to the Arts while so much emphasis is placed upon taught sciences in the education of our children.

Writing must have some purpose. To demote writing to the level of a mechanical activity which must be done at certain times, in specific places and at the bidding of an authoritarian figure is to remove at a stroke any innate motivation to write.

Becoming Familiar With Letters

Look for resources which are attractive, unusual and tactile to encourage and develop a young child's knowledge of letters. Pasta shapes in the form of letters can be weighed, played with, used in collage and art or, of course, eaten! Children will talk about the letters, identifying them, building words. So what if Philomena's tea gets cold while she is building her name on the edge of her plate? She is learning. And in how many ways? Playing with pasta shapes can involve one or more of all the senses; sight, touch, smell, taste and if you encourage the child to talk about the sound of the letter, hearing.

Sponge letters can be bought as bath toys. These curious tactile things float and when we, stick onto a smooth surface like a tiled wall or the side of the bath. Learning takes place through sight and touch, and while a child is learning about writing and reading, he is also learning about floating, sinking, friction, wet, dry…the list goes on.

Fridge magnets, or magnetic letters and boards make good toys too. These can only be used the correct way round, although of course the letter may be rotated. Whole words are available for more advanced readers, and there are grown-up versions of magnetic word sets which have an extensive vocabulary and very small letters - for those of us who like to play with words, literally! Learn about letters and science at the same time.

Suggest making model letters using plasticine or salt dough, which can be baked and decorated. The act of making a letter will teach a child about the shape of the letter, where to begin and where to end. Extend this by suggesting joining letters together.

Sand trays are often used in schools and playgroups for children to write in. Finger writing encourages free-flowing script, and in sand, mistakes do not matter - they can be rubbed out easily. At home we can extend this idea; we do not need to invest in an expensive version of a sand tray. Children can write mud in the garden, in finger paints, in spilt flour on the pastry board … and afterwards, in the bubbles as we run a bath. A trip to the seaside provides miles of sand ideal for writing in, with hands and feet... 'Sparklers' at bonfire night allow children to write their names in fire... The possibilities are endless.

At first, demonstrate writing using big movements - whole arms, legs, fingers, - for it is not until a child has control of the big movements which his body can make that the smaller motor skills can develop. Pencils are often too thin for young children to grip easily. Pencil grips can be purchased from good stationers, as can larger pencils, but they are restrictive tools for writing, especially in the early stages. Try providing wax crayons and paints, charcoal or chalks instead. These are easier for a child to handle, and encourage a free flowing formation of letters. Lots of plain paper is needed, too, and plain paper of different shapes, sizes and colours. A roll of lining paper from a DIY shop, or an end of line roll of wallpaper is an ideal cheap source of a very large piece of paper. Roll it out in the garden on a fine day, provide paints and sponges, clothe your child in swimming attire, and watch the learning happen. Stand by with a large bar of soap, a bucket and towels for the end of the activity!

Only when children are comfortable with forming letters and have had plenty of opportunity for testing skills and learning through play in this way can we expect them to begin to write in a reasonable size hand with a pencil or pen. To confront a young child with formal handwriting tasks before they have acquired this confidence is apt to cause confusion and distress and to put a child off of writing altogether.

Teaching Handwriting

There are some specific points regarding the teaching of handwriting:

✍ Children learning to write need to be correctly positioned at the table or desk. Give the child a chair and work surface of the right height.

✍ Make sure the child can see what he is doing! Is the lighting adequate? Is the example to be copied clear and easy to see? Is it presented 'straight on' in front of him, so that he can see it without having to turn his head to the right or left, or look over his shoulder?

✍ Are there suitable tools available - sharp, long pencils, fountain pens or similar ink rollerball pens and plenty of plain paper. Biros or fibre tipped pens, or pencils which are too thin or small make letter formation difficult and should not be used when teaching handwriting.

✍ Handwriting requires intense concentration, so the session should not be too long. Half an hour is more than enough for most children, and as with any skill, little and often is the key to success.

The Case For Cursive Writing

The case for cursive writing is related to the way we speak. In speech we use the whole word, not broken into different letter sounds (phonemes) or syllables. Cursive writing imitates speech as one needs to recognise the structure of the whole word before starting to write it. Advocates of the use of this style claim that its use improves spelling, speed and clarity of writing and correct use of capital letters. In fact, although it is seldom taught to children in mainstream school it is often successfully used by teachers of dyslexics and those with specific learning difficulties as a recognised aid to language and writing.

Cursive writing can be used from the very start, abandoning the 'sticks and circles' printing style so often found in nursery and infants schools altogether. The standard approach to the teaching of writing is puzzling. Why do we teach our children to write in print and on plain paper as infants, spend time and effort in teaching them to write all over again in a joined up style and on lined paper in the junior KS2 years, and then expect them to write a decent letter on plain paper when they apply for a job? Surely this makes writing unnecessarily complicated before one adds the skills of spelling, grammar and even the basic use of capital letters.

There are several styles of joined up writing which are taught in schools, but true cursive writing is rare. During the latter part of the 1960s the cursive writing style which we learnt in school went right out of educational fashion. Recently there has been some movement back towards the teaching of cursive writing. The great advantage of the style is that, almost without exception, all the letters join up. Whole words can and should be written without the pen leaving the paper; the letters *i* and *j* are dotted and *t* crossed only when the word is finished.

The examples given illustrate the lower and upper case alphabet in the cursive writing style. Notice that all letters have a 'foot' and a 'tail', a start and an end, so they naturally want to join on to another letter and encourage a flowing style. When teaching writing, use plain paper, crayons, paints and fountain pens which will aid the development of a free flowing script. Pencils are usually thin and make the user grip hard, constricting movement. Likewise, lined paper inhibits the natural formation of the letters and words. Handwriting books with lots of lines and sometimes in different colours are available from stationery shops and these can be useful to refine handwriting, but should not be considered when a child is just starting to write.

The cursive letter 's' does not join very naturally, but this will come with practice. Some of the capital letters do look rather fancy in their style, and can always be replaced by standard print forms, but I have found that children like to use these rather elaborate letters and feel quite a sense of achievement when they can write them.

Question why you want your child to write and what qualities in the writing of other people you most admire, and what qualities annoy you. Speed and clarity may be of the utmost importance if examinations are to be taken, whereas enjoyment of the art of writing might be more pressing considerations for a young child.

Computers And Voice-Recognition Technology

Many people have access to personal computers. Especially if linked to the Internet, the computer is an invaluable tool for the home-educating family. Having a word processor can really encourage reluctant writers. Children often find forming letters demanding, both on time and concentration. Some are constantly disappointed that writing takes a lot of effort and fails to look as neat or tidy as they would wish. Other children seem drawn towards anything resembling a keyboard, and will happily write for a long time using a keyboard, when they would not attempt to do any writing at all with a pen

Children have not inherited any phobia of the computer technology, and they will need to be computer literate - life demands that we use keyboards in most activities, and computer literacy is a pre-requisite for many forms of employment. Of course it is desirable for children to be taught to write by hand, and to develop an attractive, legible style of handwriting, but they also need to be able to use a keyboard. Perhaps we should be looking at the teaching of touch-typing alongside the teaching of writing.

Word processors specifically for young children are available, and have been used in schools for about fifteen years. Our children have had no difficulty in writing with the same word processor software with which this book was written, and we have not seen the need to invest in any specialist software.

Voice Recognition Technology (VRT) enables the computer to recognise the spoken word, and transfer it to the screen and then the written page. For dyslexic and dyspraxic children, or those with some physical disability, this must be as a gift from God. Geoff Harrison, who is severely dyslexic, has found that VRT has changed his life. With it he is able to communicate using written text for the first time in his life - in fact, he works in the production of Education Now's magazine, News and Review.

These days we are surrounded by more opportunities for literacy than ever before. Curiously, we are developing more ways of overcoming illiteracy too - we no longer need to be able to read in the widely accepted sense to be able to understand the messages of the advertisers; writing do longer depends upon the ability to form letters on a page with a pen. But these skills are not yet completely outdated - far from it! Literacy is important, for survival, in order to secure employment, and for leisure. The need for literacy remains constant, and it is the duty of responsible home-educating parents to make every opportunity for learning language in all its forms available to their children.

Number

We have chosen to refer to Number, not Mathematics or Arithmetic, as it is the fundamental comprehension of number which we are concerned with here. A good grounding in the understanding of number is essential; without it confusion is likely to develop and compound as more complex processes are introduced. This section gives some considerations which wissians may find helpful when embarking on the subject of numeracy. It is the result of practical experience and observations of children over many years rather than an academic study in the psychology surrounding the teaching and learning of number skills.

Talking

Child/adult interaction is the single most important factor in the learning process which children have at home and which disappears immediately they start school. The fact that as home educators we are able to continue talking to our children and listening to them gives us a distinct advantage over the school system. The value of talking cannot be over-emphasised, and this applies to every subject area, every aspect of the learning process. Before anything else can happen, talking and listening must occur if understanding is to be achieved.

An understanding of number and number operations can be identified even before a child has developed language. A mother who counts her baby's socks and shoes as she puts them on him, who says, "one, two.." as she puts the infant's arms into his sleeves, is teaching the child number, and the child is learning. Playing with a pre-language child can reveal how much grasp of number operations is already in place. A child at this age can be asked to find 'one more' or to 'take one away', and even before the child is able to speak, their comprehension of language may be sufficiently developed to show an understanding of the action required. Throughout learning, and especially in the early stages of numeracy, dialogue remains vital. Before any attempt is made at completing written tasks in number children must be given plenty of opportunity to develop, consolidate and reinforce ideas and concepts. Only when the wissian is absolutely certain that an idea is fully understood should the learner write down the results.

Plato defined learning as dialogue, and thought as the inner dialogue of the soul with itself: it can be argued that we cannot improve on these definitions.
Ruth Merttens, Teaching Numeracy

Counting

Many children develop the ability to count from an early age. They do so by mimicking, learning a sequence by rote, naturally or by being taught by other children or adults who have greater expertise. Thus, a child of two can count to ten, twenty, a hundred... but the ability to count does not equate to understanding of number.

Counting is nevertheless an important skill; it relates to sequencing, memory, learning through imitation - all vital skills which become the tools of the developing learner. There are good counting games and songs which parents naturally use with their babies:

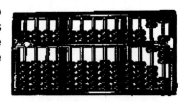

♫ One, two, three four five, Once I caught a fish alive...

♫ This little piggy went to market...

♫ Knick-knack Paddy-Whack...

These are all good, sound desirable activities which equip the growing child with building blocks of knowledge. The toddler may be able to understand the concept of adding one more, or taking one away, or sharing. The ability to deal with these very basic number operations requires an understanding of number over the ability to repeat and sequence. Grasp of the concept of the 'number line', the sequence of numbers in a pattern, is crucial for young children in the learning of number and number operations.

Understanding Number

As a general rule, children are unable to comprehend number much beyond their own chronological age until around about the age when they change their teeth. This may seem a curious statement, and it is based upon observation rather than quantifiable scientific research. Of course there will be exceptions - the five-year-old who passes A-level maths, for example. The philosophy which underlies the Steiner approach to education reflects the physical developmental stages in children and also acknowledges the 'change of teeth' as a milestone in intellectual development.

Young children who are able to count well, forwards and backwards, may experience some difficulty with even simple number operations using numbers greater than, say, two years beyond their own age. If you are educating your own child at home this simple rule of thumb may save much anguish and concern when beginning to teach number. It provides an answer to questions like, "He can count up to fifty, so why can't he work out what 24 and 16 are?"

The first concepts that children are expected to grasp are the most difficult - the first sequence of numbers. There seems to be no relationship between the numbers up to ten - they form a sequence which must simply be remembered, learnt by heart. Having learnt them, the pattern of numbers begins to become apparent. Small children, however, seem to have the ability to take the information in without question and in most cases, retain it. As with language, the rudiments of number are accepted in a small child without question and without the need for explanation or logic.

Experience

Children seem to have a need for moving objects when counting in order to make sense of the count. This is the developmental stage which the psychologist Piaget identified as the *concrete operational skills*, that is, the use of real objects in learning to understand, in this case, number. Children in infant schools are given bricks and beads to assist in learning to count and to execute basic number operations.

Home educators do not need to equip their homes with all the paraphernalia of the infant classroom. The opportunities for young children to count in a meaningful way are many and varied at home. Counting tins into the cupboard, potatoes into the saucepan, tomatoes into the bag etc. all provide valid practice at the same skills children use in a formal classroom setting with bricks and worksheets. The difference is crucial: at home, by counting in practical work the activity is meaningful. To the child at school the purpose of number operations remains unclear. Experience in handling numbers is available, but limited; all-important dialogue even more so. To the home-educated child there is a reason behind the activity: *we need five yoghurts because there are five of us and we would all like one!* Home-educated children have the great advantage over their schooled counterparts in the early stages of learning.

Aids To Learning

Tools are necessary if number processes are to be understood. Human beings have ten fingers - we carry our own calculator with us all the while. Why not use it? It costs nothing to run, and hopefully, is never lost. Encourage the learner to use it.

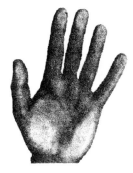

There are many ways of using fingers to assist counting. For advanced finger users, counting up to 1023 on ten fingers is possible using a binary method. Using patterns made by moving fingers, the nine-times table is made simple. The hands have been used as mathematical tools and memory aids since the beginning of man's numeracy - the Imperial system of measurement based an inch upon the distance between the top of the thumb and the first joint; a span was the distance across the palm of the outstretched hand, a cubit the length between the elbow and the tip of the longest finger; a yard the distance from the tip of the outstretched arm to the side of the body to the tip of the nose when facing forward, etc. Market traders selling cloth used this method of measuring out the fabric. Metrication has in all likelihood, put an end to such practice and children in the UK now have no means of 'guesstimating' length other than learning what a centimetre looks like.

Calculators

The part that calculators take in education continues to be hotly disputed. Policies vary between utter reliance and complete bans.

By using calculators, time is not being wasted on long sums where a result is needed for a specific purpose, rather than the sum as an exercise in itself. Planning a complex calculation for a machine does promote logical thought. In addition, it is fun. A child's delight in pressing buttons to produce a response is being pandered to, here.

Reliance on the machine, on the other hand, leads to the situation where the learner becomes unable to do the sum if the calculator is not available. The logic and methods of long multiplication and division are reinforced by usage.

The happy medium is when the learner is able to use either method, choosing the calculator only for speed. It is important, when using a calculator, to make an estimate of the result before starting the calculation, otherwise a miskeying may go unnoticed.

Geography

The study of geography as a subject encompasses the concepts of spatial awareness - where am I in relation to my home, town, county, country etc., the shape and formation of the earth, and the economics and politics of the countries of the world. To reduce it to its simplest form, one can study geography in three ways - from the largest to the smallest (macro-micro), from the smallest to the largest (micro-macro) or a combination of both. It is the second option which appears preferable to take, as study in this way can begin with experience - in fact it can start at home, with ideas as small as the spatial layout of the dining table, the geography of the sitting room - and work up to concepts and ideas about the town, country, globe. This is not, it seems, the way of teaching geography in schools at the moment, where a 'compare and contrast' approach is the order of the day. A young child might study the local river or lake one day, and coral reefs the next.

Of course, knowledge of different parts of the world, different cultures, climates and cultures is important and should be given due consideration by the home educator. Geography on a global scale, however, only becomes meaningful if the learner has a good grounding in local knowledge, based upon first hand experience. Home-educating families can use their freedom of movement and liberation from the prescribed curriculum to the best advantage, making every effort to take the learner out into the environment where geography can be experienced in the most effective, holistic way - through the soles of the boots.

- ⊕ Use the environment

- ⊕ Work outwards from home to the rest of the world, relating experiences to what is already understood.

- ⊕ Seek first-hand evidence, ask questions, notice the positions of different buildings, landscapes. Talk about what you observe, and try to find reasons for your observations.

Science

Much science can be gleaned not from deep scientific knowledge and taught formulae, but from encouragement in questioning and use of a scientific approach to thinking which builds on knowledge which has already been acquired. Observation, action, recording, reflection is the basis of the cycle of learning in science, to which we can add questioning, information gathering and data collection/analysis. Science of all kinds can be learnt very effectively at home without any need for a fully equipped laboratory, chemicals or specialist measuring and recording equipment. Until the study becomes quite specialist, at GCSE or A-level standard, the kind of  equipment which can be found in most kitchens and bathrooms is perfectly adequate - funnels, scales, timers, a magnifying glass, jam-jars and collecting tins/tubs, etc. Science is one of the areas of the curriculum which has enjoyed a huge government-backed push in the last few years, being given the status of one of the first core areas of the National Curriculum. Consequently there is a vast range of good scientific material easily available in the High Street book shops and educational toy shops. Such specialist things as microscopes, project kits and easy-to-understand teaching resources are not difficult to acquire. These days, the non-specialist need not feel daunted by the prospect of teaching basic science. The resources are plentiful, and once again, the home educator can begin at home using the everyday science within the home environment.

✓ Make full and free use of the materials and equipment available to you.

✓ Develop an enquiring mind, asking why, rather than blindly accepting information.

✓ Listen and talk with the learner, encouraging him to ask questions. It is not the role of the wissian to have a ready answer to all scientific questions, but to know where to begin to find the answers.

✓ Practice observing and recording in a logical way. Take time to reflect and discuss, and try making predictions and testing theories.

History

A study of the past does not need to be boring, dependant upon learning names and dates, battles, kings and queens by heart and regurgitating them for an examination. In history, as much as with anything else, the home educator is able to use the environment, searching for clues to discover more about how people lived in the past, and how their lives have affected present day life in one's own community. In the study of History, detective skills really come to the fore, so here is a chance to be really inquisitive. The sense of achievement gained when discovering something for oneself is immense, and history provides that opportunity. Start as close to home as possible with familiar objects or places. Perhaps you own some item of interest and antiquity which could give rise to an investigation. Maybe your own house or street is old, and records could be searched which would enable you to build up a picture of the local history. Is there someone who featured in history who lived or worked in your town? Is there a monument, or some antique feature which could be used as a starting point for a historical investigation - a horse trough, water pump or well for example. The parish church and churchyard can also be a fruitful start. The school approach to studying history through using books as the source of both inspiration and evidence in the absence of opportunity to use the environment can make the subject deadly dull. Home educators, however, can and should use the environment at every opportunity. First-hand, material sources of historical evidence can really bring the subject to life.

- Use primary sources of information - physical evidence from the environment, oral evidence from talking and listening to people, and build upon those.

- Record findings and the sources from which they come.

- Develop investigative skills, and build upon the local and personal knowledge of history to accumulate greater knowledge of different times and peoples.

Art

Art can be therapeutic and expressive, allowing children to convey messages through form and colour which they may not be able to express in any other way. Young children use art in this way all the time, and it is only as they grow and recognise pictures that they become preoccupied with shape, perspective and light. There are very few rules in art. Provide as much paper as possible and unlimited opportunity for use of colour on paper. You will need a good cheap supply of paper and a variety of art mediums and tools - several kinds of paints and brushes, sponges, rollers etc. Find out about the colour wheel and learn which colours go together well and which do not, use contrasts of light and dark colours and encourage children to mix their own colours from the primary colours plus black and white. Perspective can be introduced by pointing out that things far away appear smaller than things which are nearby. Colours change with distance too - the farther away, the less intense the colour and vice versa. The last rule which needs to be introduced is *draw what you see, not what you think you see*. Some people see shapes as patches of light and sometimes thinking in this way helps when attempting to put shape and form on paper. Finally, encourage the learner to aim to feel satisfied with the artwork he produces. It is of greater importance that children feel a sense of enjoyment and achievement in art than that they produce a masterpiece.

- Give access to as many and varied materials for Art as possible.
- Try out different ideas, copying other people's ideas and developing them as well as trying out your own.
- Watch artists at work, and observe how different techniques produce different effects.
- Do not be afraid to make mistakes, to throw work away or to try again. Aim to be satisfied with a piece of work, rather than really pleased.

CDT

This area of the curriculum used to be called 'craft' - a term which still brings raffia mats and cross-stitch embroidery on canvas to mind for many of today's parents. In schools today, CDT activities hover uncomfortably somewhere between what one might expect to see on Blue Peter - (an empty washing-up liquid bottle, sticky back plastic and rubber solution glue) and some fairly intricate high-tech models controlled by a child-written computer program. Preoccupation with the so-called basic skills in schools has squeezed out much opportunity for arts and crafts. Although the woodworking tools, Lego Technic, empty yoghurt pots and egg boxes can still be found in classroom, they are frequently relegated to a position in the back of a stock cupboard rather than occupying pride of place in the primary classroom as they did ten years ago.

This is a shame. Craft presents yet another way in which children can learn, and it is often the children who are poor readers and reluctant writers who excel in the field of arts and crafts. At home, making working models and exploring design and function can be unpopular, as these activities demand space and time, and inevitably create a mess. It is not always possible to have the dining table completely taken over by one child who wants to build a papier maché pig, or to find space for the model of the Nile, complete with pyramids and palm trees to be displayed. Space in an ordinary home is often at a premium, especially if there is a large family to be home-educated, so CDT activities may not be as readily available as we would like. It may be prudent to wait for a fine day when children can work in the garden before some tasks are attempted, or to take advantage of children's workshop sessions at libraries, arts centres or Scrapstores and book the children in for these.

Making things depends on a supply of materials. Collecting empty cartons, packaging, pots and jars takes time and space, so availability and storage can be a problem. If one can plan ahead, however, start collecting in advance and be disciplined enough to throw unwanted craft materials away after the event, CDT can be one of the most valuable activities for dialogue, interaction between all the age groups and fun in the home educator's world.

- Encourage play with model making materials of all kinds, clay, plasticine, wood, packaging etc.

- When embarking on a larger project, take time to plan which materials will be needed and find a source.

🖼 Remember that craft projects take time and space to complete and display. Make arrangements for this before starting a project.

🖼 CDT links well with both Art and Science and language. Work with the learner, assisting him to solve problems by asking questions of him rather than giving the answers.

Music

Music provides the inspiration and the opportunity for free expression in children, through participation in making music and response to the sound. It is sometimes only through response to music that any expression can manifest itself.

No specialist knowledge or ability is required to listen to music. It costs little - most families have a radio, tape recorder or CD player, and access to a record library. This is often the area in which the adults can first begin to extend their own education in a conscious way, by deliberately choosing to listen to music which they might never have considered before. Music, more than anything else, is transitory in nature - it is there, and it is gone. If you did not enjoy it, you need never listen to it again. Switch it off, walk away, make a mental note never to attend a concert which includes a particular work. By broadening one's experience of music, however, one may be pleasantly surprised. Who could have anticipated the sudden rise in popularity and appreciation of grand opera arias which followed the Italian World Cup? It is not necessary to be able to read music or to be a musician for music to become part of the home educator's way of life. Listening, even at the level of having some background music on whilst other activities are going on, extends education through hearing. Melodies and rhythms will be absorbed, almost unconsciously, and recognised again.

Children may find some sounds particularly appealing and wish to learn more about an instrument. If they do, the onus falls upon the parent to assist with this. Music shops often have loan schemes for musical instruments, as do music schools, and in some areas the LEA will allow home educators to borrow instruments and have lessons from the music teachers who work within the authority for similar rates to the children in school. Libraries often keep a list of music teachers who give private lessons, and there may be established music groups which welcome and teach children to sing or play, perhaps connected with a local church or community, like a brass band or community band or dance group.

Home educators do not have to study in silence or near silence, or to categorise music into a special slot or time of day. Music does appear as a separate subject on the scheme, and as part of a balanced education, perhaps there is a place for parents and children to sit quietly together and listen to and discuss a piece of music as part of the day's study pattern. Some children may wish to take that time to practise an instrument, or to make an instrument, to use music as a source of inspiration for Art or Language. Dancing or playing certainly cannot be skills which are divorced from numeracy, as counting and understanding time are crucial to both the music and movement.

♪ Use the teaching of music as part of home education to extend your own knowledge of the subject.

♪ Listen and experience as many different kinds of music as possible, not restricting it to any particular music styles.

♪ Do not be afraid to reject music which you do not like, but do give new music a chance, and do discuss what you hear.

♪ Find out where you can hear more music, or 'meet' musical instruments. If your child wishes to play an instrument, match the child to the instrument. Do not be talked into taking a course of music lessons for an instrument in which the child has little interest because everyone starts on it, or because it supposedly gives a good musical grounding.

♪ Encourage an amount of discipline in learning an instrument, but be wary of insisting that lessons continue if the child no longer enjoys playing the instrument. No one learns when they are unhappy.

Marking Children's Work

Most LEAs expect to see work marked, as in school. For home-based educators (and for many teachers) marking work serves only as a check that the study has been pitched at the correct level for the child, and that the task required has been understood. A teacher should never need to put rows of crosses against incorrect answers - if a child does not understand what he is practising he should not be asked to attempt it. With home-based education the amount of time spent on repetitive written exercises is minimal compared with that spent on similar activities in school. The amount of work which requires marking is also far less. In terms of home-based education, where children are rarely tested or allocated grades, marking comes to mean correcting - a task which is meaningless as an aid to learning unless it is done in the presence of the child. Correcting a piece of work may mean reading through a script, discussing the content, grammar and language used, checking that it makes sense and conveys the message which the child intended, working through spellings which the child could be expected to be able to work out or know but has got wrong, finding or giving the correct spellings of words which the child could not be expected to know, and, in a similar way, checking for punctuation. Correcting a mathematical exercise may involve checking the answers to a set of sums, working through incorrect calculations with the child, or working through problems together when the child has arrived at the wrong answer.

The differences between home-based and school education cannot be stressed enough. Most of us have been through the school system, and our recollections of that are naturally our benchmark for standards and methods which we impart to our own children. Any thoughts which you have about marking of your children's work at home will form a crucial part of your own educational philosophy. The central question which must be addressed when developing a philosophy is "Why am I doing/requiring/teaching/encouraging this?" Every home-educating family will have a different philosophy and a different attitude to marking and correcting written work. Although most LEAs set some store by seeing marked work as 'evidence' of ongoing education, in reality diligent marking of written work hardly qualifies as evidence of education! Think carefully, consider your reasons for marking work and the strategy you will use, and be prepared to justify them to your child, your partner, your family and if necessary to an outsider or LEA officer.

Why Mark Children's Work?

There are probably going to be a variety of reasons for marking and these will affect the way in which work is corrected. For instance, if a child has written a letter to a friend or relative, a parent may require spellings and grammar to be correct, content to be appropriate and the letter to be set out properly on the page. It would not be unreasonable to correct a first attempt together with the child and ask him to rewrite the letter correctly before sending it off. Imagine, however, that a child has worked through a set of grammatical exercises in which he is required to identify, say, the verb in each sentence. He has completed the given task correctly, but has made a few slips in basic punctuation. Would it be appropriate to mark every error and request that the whole exercise be written out again? Or would pointing out the errors in punctuation be sufficient? In a case like this, parents and teachers may need to consider external factors like the time of day the work was done, the interest level of the task, the general health and alertness of the child, and the motivation of the child to succeed at the task.

When To Mark Work

In school, written work is handed in to the teacher who marks it, often after school or at home in the evenings, and hands it back at the next opportunity. There is little if any opportunity for discussion of the marking or the grade. Even in primary schools this system is quite commonly employed, yet its worth as far as learning is concerned is very questionable.

At home, written work can be corrected immediately and with the student present to comment, listen and discuss any changes which are made. Correcting or at least acknowledging completed work immediately gives positive immediate reinforcement - an effective learning strategy for the pupil, and less time consuming for the tutor. The *'mark as you go'* approach is attempted in some schools but with the best will in the world it is not always possible to work this way with classes of 30+. At home with even the largest family it is hard to see how this method can be improved upon.

Keep a pen or pencil with you all the while, so that you can stop anything else you happen to be doing when a child comes with a piece of work, and put acknowledge written work immediately. This means a lot to a child, and the very action of making the mark reassures you that you have seen the completed task.

How To Mark Work

Personal recollection of marking at school is often that of efforts at written work being returned covered in red biro ticks or crosses, perhaps with some meaningless comment like *'well done'* or *'careless work'* and a grade at the bottom of the page.

We are led to believe that the red pen and the term *'marking'* came from antiquity, when children were literally marked, probably with a stick, for mistakes in their work, the red signifying the blood which was drawn. A different pen from that which the child has used will distinguish the marks on the paper which have been made by another person, but red is not the ideal colour.

Question how to mark work and why. If it is to provide positive reinforcement, a virtual pat on the back for each correct answer, only ticks need be given. Crosses against incorrect responses only serve to give a negative response; they are unnecessary. Correct answers can be ticked, incorrect answers should be questioned, but as far as marking is concerned they can be left alone. When working with an individual writing lengthy comments on work are pointless - the wissian can say what needs to be said at the time. A *'well done'* or some stamp of approval like a smiley face or star on the work of a child to signify your pleasure is often reward enough for a child, but can be incorporated into a system of rewards which add to the motivation to work carefully and make some effort.

A Democratic Approach

In all cases of home-education, a democratic approach to acknowledgement of written work is possible. Many children value some mark of approval being placed upon their written work; this is especially true of children who have experienced the school system - after all, it is what school has trained them to expect. A system of marking can be much more comprehensive and effective at home. In the first place it can be negotiated and agreed between the wissian and the learner so that all parties know and understand the value of the rewards indicated and the meanings of the corrections given.

Respect of the child's work is a key factor; before taking a pen to a child's work a parent should seek the permission of the child, who is the owner of the script. It may be that discussion of the errors made will be sufficient in terms of learning. Sometimes a piece of written work may represent a great effort on the part of the child, who, although aware that it will not be perfect, is satisfied to leave it as it stands, warts and all. To indicate corrections in some cases can be destructive and damaging. At other times marking and correcting mistakes can be both appropriate and effective in the learning process. The child will often recognise such occasions and actually want his work marked.

✓ Marking of work should be done only as part of an ongoing effective learning strategy.

✓ It should be a democratic process, agreed and understood by all involved.

✓ If done at all it should be carried out as soon as possible after work has been completed, and in the presence of the child.

✓ It should be specific - focused upon particular points of learning, and never destructive. As a general rule if a pleasant, constructive comment cannot be made it is better to make no mark at all.

Chapter Nine

Finally…

Teachers open the door, but you must enter by yourself.

Chinese Proverb

How Will I Know If It Worked?

League tables published in the national press tell us how the government feel education is to be measured. Claims by books and computer software sales literature suggest that education can be accelerated and that it is desirable to do so.

Education came first, then examinations were introduced to test the efficacy of the education. So much significance was attached in people's minds that education has now been tailored to the point where certificates and grades have now become the objectives of education. The tail is wagging the dog, and we reach the position where people with high academic qualifications cannot boil an egg, read a railway timetable or estimate a yard.

Commercial enterprises wasted no time in exploiting this obsession with examinations. The phrase *"supports the National Curriculum"* is used as an advertising line, as vacuous as *"washes whiter"* or *"nothing works better"*. Toys are marketed as being educational.

All play is educational, whether it uses a Star Wars light sabre or a "Talking Whiz Kid Einstein Mouse" (not joking! Both these items are in the Argos catalogue). The difference is that one encourages imaginative play, the other continues the narrowness of schooling at home. You may, like us, discourage toy weapons, but from what we have seen of recent real-life warfare it seems that the deadliest of weapons are now controlled from a computer keyboard anyway.

The other aspect of examinations and grading is the unhealthy competitiveness engendered between parents, and the implicit need to achieve. Home education does not avoid this - in fact its very flexibility permits accelerated learning to the extent that the majority of very young university entrants seem to be home-educated. Learning can certainly be accelerated to the detriment of a normal development, but that is not necessarily desirable. Images of the goose stuffed to make pâté de foie gras come to mind; children are stuffed with learning until they are completely bloated. Is that the final aim of education?

Real education cannot be measured. As with the whole of life, you only get one shot at the twelve years of compulsory education, so a direct comparison of home education against conventional schooling is impossible. Maybe there will be times when you ask yourself, *"did I do the right thing in taking him out of school?"* Knowing the alternative, however, you might equally have said, *"would I have done better at home?"*

This is what parenting is all about. You will probably never know the answer. Just ask yourself: Is your child happy? Can he see further than the classroom? Does he have an open-minded and intelligent approach to his learning?

And can he boil an egg?

Appendix A

Glossary Of Terms

cursive   joined-up writing, each letter ending on the base line with an appropriate joining stroke.

Digraph   two letters giving one sound, e.g. th, or, ow

EWO   Education Welfare Officer

grapheme   the letter or combination of letters used to represent a sound

holistic   complete and self-contained, making use of all the senses

Home Education Manager   given different titles by different LEAs, this is the education advisor responsible for monitoring home-educating families. Usually experienced in the teaching profession.

LEA   Local Education Authority

Ofsted   Office for Standards in Education, a non-ministerial government department, independent of the Department for Education and Employment. Ofsted was set up on 1.9.92., and is officially the Office of Her Majesty's Chief Inspector of Schools in England.

Phoneme   the sound in speech, represented by a grapheme

SEN   Special Educational Needs

THRASS   Teaching Handwriting, Reading And Spelling Skills

wissian   see page 123

Appendix B

Resources

Support

Advisory Centre for Education

Independent national watchdog which gives free advice and support to parents.

ACE Ltd.
1b Aberdeen Studios
22 - 24 Highbury Grove
London
N5 2DQ
Tel. 0171 354 8321 (Mon. - Fri., 2 - 5pm)

Childline

Freephone 0800 1111

Children's Legal Centre

Publish the Education Rights Handbook. Advice line Mon. - Fri., 2 - 5 p.m.

University of Essex
Wivenhoe Park
Colchester
Essex
CO4 3SQ
Tel. 01206 - 873820

Choice In Education

Choice In Education publish an independent monthly newsletter for home educators.

PO Box 20284
London
NW1 3WY

Education Now

Publishes information and books about all aspects of alternative education in Britain and abroad. Members receive a quarterly newsletter and discount offers on other publications from the Educational Heretics Press.

Education Now
113 Arundel Drive,
Bramcote Hills,
Nottingham
NG9 3FQ
www.gn.apc.org/educationnow

Education Otherwise

The most well-known home education support group, EO is now over twenty years old. It provides a wealth of information about the legal side of home education and has members all over Britain and contacts across the world. Each county has a co-ordinator, and meetings, workshops, camps and activities are organised for members. Membership of E.O. provides contact with other home educators and contact with an organisation made up of experienced home educators who can be called upon for help and advice.

Education Otherwise
PO Box 7420
London
N9 9SG
Recorded message: 0891 518303
Emergency number: 0870 7300074
Email: enquiries@education-otherwise.org
http://e-o.users.netlink.co.uk/mindex.htm

Family Rights Group

Support for families where children are in contact with Social Services.

> The Print House
> 18 Ashwin Street
> London
> E8 3DL
> Tel. 0171 923 2628
> Advice line 0171 249 0008

Herald

Formed in 1997, Herald (Home Education Resources and Learning Development) offer practical advice on designing individual schemes of study covering eight main areas of the curriculum. Herald produce three topic packs a year, together with teaching notes, resource lists and special offers on books or teaching equipment which is not easily available in shops.

> Herald
> Kelda Cottage
> Lydbrook
> Gloucester
> GL17 9SX
> Tel. 01594 - 861107
> E-mail: herald@altavista.net
> http://www.homeeducation.co.uk

Home Education Advisory Service

This organisation does a similar job to Education Otherwise. It publishes a lot of material which may particularly appeal to the families of dyslexic and Special Educational Needs children. Newer than E.O., it is run by home educators and produces excellent informative material which would be of interest to any home-educating family.

> Home Education Advisory Service
> PO Box 98
> Welwyn Garden City
> Herts
> AL8 6AN
> Tel: 01707 371854
> Email: admin@heas.org.uk
> http://www.heas.org.uk

Human Scale Education

Formed to promote and extend the small schools movement, HES also back moves for Flexi-schooling and alternatives to conventional schools. There are several 'small schools' across the country now, and more opening all the time.

> Human Scale Education
> Fiona Carnie
> 96 Carlingcott
> Bath
> BA2 8AW

Kidscape

Keeping Kids Safe, especially from bullying.

> 152 Buckingham Palace Road
> London
> SW1W 9TR
> Tel. 0171 730 3300

NSPCC

24 hour child protection Helpline

> Freephone 0800 800 500

The Open University

> Walton Hall,
> Milton Keynes,
> MK7 6AA
> Tel: 01908 274066
> http://www.open.ac.uk/frames.html

Other Resources

Parent Network

Support for families. Has locally based groups.

44-46 Caversham Road
London
NW5 2DS
Tel. 0171 485 8535

Parentline UK

Runs a network of telephone lines for parents under stress.

01702 559900

Schoolhouse

The support group for Scottish home educators.

Schoolhouse Home Education Association
93 Blacklock Crescent
Dundee
DD4 8EE
01382 646964

WES Home School

Established to support parents who work abroad and take their children with them, WES is the oldest support group. It provides structured work plans tailor made to individual requirements and geared to the National Curriculum. Students are assigned a personal tutor who sets the work and gives guidance on curriculum development. WES no longer work only with children who are resident abroad but with home educators in Britain too. If and when children return to school WES provide a written report about the child's progress and details of the work which has been set for him.

WES Home School
World-wide Education Service
Balgrave House
17 Balgrave Street,
Reading,
Berkshire.
RG1 1QA
Tel. 0118 - 958 9993

Oxford University Press

Oxford Reading Tree, Fuzzbuzz

Primary Marketing Department
Great Clarendon Street
Oxford
OX2 6DP
Tel. 01865 556767

Centre For The Teaching Of Reading

University of Reading
School of Education
29, Eastern Avenue
Reading
Berkshire

British Dyslexia Association

98, London Road
Reading
Berkshire RG1 5AU
Tel. 01734 - 668271

The Dyslexia Institute

133 Gresham Road
Staines
Middlesex TW18 2AJ
Tel. 01784 - 463851

Read And Write Together

Free booklet for parents. Up to date information, tips on teaching reading and writing, games, etc.

BBC Learning Support 1998
White City
201 Wood Lane
London W12 7TS

Basic Skills Agency

Tel. 0800 700 987

National Year of Reading

DfEE Publication. Free booklet

Tel.0845 60 222 60, quoting ref. Number NYR2PG

AVP Software

Produce reading software for PC, Acorn and Apple computers. Include support material for BBC Look and Read.

School Hill Centre
CHEPSTOW
Monmouthshire
NP6 5PH

THRASS

Collins Educational Freepost GW5078
Bishopbriggs
Glasgow
GW64 1BR
0141 306 3484

Ginn and Company Ltd.,

Ginn Reading 360

Prenbendal House,
Parsons Fee
Aylesbury,
Bucks.
HB20 2QZ

H.E.R.O. Books

Home Education Reading Opportunities

58 Portland Road,
Hove,
East Sussex
BN3 5DL
Tel. 01273 775560

Appendix C

Picture Credits

Thomas Brooks	House (p.36)
Snap Magor-Elliott	Baobab Tree (p.9)
Mary Ann Rose	Chalkboard (p.61)
Ben Stanbrook	Pig (p.41), Telephone (p.88), Letter (p.89), Washing Machine (p.109), Englishman's Home (p.118), Cup Of Tea (p.119), Pyramids and Sphinx (p.172)
Joe Stanbrook	Juggler (p.13), Castle (p.18), Sport (p.40), Scrapbook (p.102), Calendar (p.104), Clock (p.145), Reading Together (p.171)
Kester Stanbrook	Spiders (p.57)
Polly Stanbrook	Family (p.8), Queen (p.12), Hospital (p.16), House (p.131)
Holly Thomas	House (front cover)
Hope Thomas	Slide In Garden (p.70)

Appendix D

Bibliography

ALMOND, David; Skellig, Hodder Children's Books, 1998, ISBN 0340 71600 2

BONDI, H; Why I Don't Like Religion in Theory And Practice Of Regressive Education (R Meighan), Educational Heretics Press 1993, ISBN 0 9518022 3 2

BRADLEY, C; Home Education Is Total Commitment in Learning From Home Based Education (Ed. R. Meighan), Education Now 1992; ISBN 1 871526 06 X

BROWN, T; Play And Number In Teaching Numeracy - Maths In The Primary Classroom (Ed. R. Merttens), Scholastic Primary Professional Bookshelf 1997, ISBN 0 590 53429 7

CASTLE, E.B.; Ancient Education And Today, Penguin Books Ltd 1961

COLES, M; Discouraging Fluent Reading in Theory And Practice Of Regressive Education (R Meighan), Educational Heretics Press 1993, ISBN 0 9518022 3 2

COX, B; Making Home Education A Normal And Available Option For All in Learning From Home Based Education (Ed. R. Meighan), Education Now 1992; ISBN 1 871526 06 X

DANIELS, J.C. & DIACK, H; The Standard Reading Tests, Hart Davis Educational 1977

DAVIS, Roland D & BRAUN, Eldon M; The Gift Of Dyslexia, Souvenir Press 1994, ISBN 0 285 63281 7

DICKENSON, P; Could Do Better, Arrow Books Ltd 1982, ISBN 0 09 928320 4

DONALDSON, M; Children's Minds, Fontana Press (Harper Collins) 1978

DOWNING, W; Making It Work Both In And Out Of School in Learning From Home Based Education (Ed. R. Meighan), Education Now 1992; ISBN 1 871526 06 X

EBBUTTT, S; Assessing Numeracy In Teaching Numeracy - Maths In The Primary Classroom (Ed. R. Merttens), Scholastic Primary Professional Bookshelf 1997, ISBN 0 590 53429 7

EMBLEN, V; Bilingual Children Learning Number In Teaching Numeracy - Maths In The Primary Classroom (Ed. R. Merttens), Scholastic Primary Professional Bookshelf 1997, ISBN 0 590 53429 7

FORTUNE-WOOD, J; Doing It Their Way, Educational Heretics Press 2000, ISBN 1/871526-42-6

GAMMAGE, P; Taller by being measured in Theory And Practice Of Regressive Education (R Meighan), Educational Heretics Press 1993, ISBN 0 9518022 3 2

HARBER, C; Democratic Learning And Learning Democracy, Education Now 1992, ISBN 1 871526 09 4

HOLT, J; How Children Learn; Penguin Books Ltd. 1967

HORNSBY, B & SHEAR, F; Alpha To Omega, Heinemann Educational 1993, ISBN 0 435 10388 1

LINDENFIELD, G; Confident Children, Thorsons (Harper Collins) 1994, ISBN 07225 2824 8

MACLURE, J. STUART; Educational Documents, England and Wales 1816 to the present day, Methuen & Co Ltd. 1974

MARTIN, C; The Holistic Educators; Educational Heretics Press 1997, ISBN 1 900219 08 5

MEIGHAN, R; The Next Learning System, And Why Home-Schoolers Are Trailblazers; Educational Heretics Press 1997, ISBN 1-900219-04-2

MEIGHAN, R; John Holt: Personalised Education And The Reconstruction Of Schooling, Educational Heretics Press 1995, ISBN 0 9518022 8 3

MEIGHAN, R; Theory And Practice Of Regressive Education, Educational Heretics Press 1993, ISBN 0 9518022 3 2

MEIGHAN, R; Learning From Home Based Education, Education Now 1992, ISBN 1 871526 06 X

MEIGHAN, R & TOOGOOD, P; Anatomy Of Choice In Education, Education Now 1992, ISBN 1 871526 07 8

MEIGHAN, J; Hijack Of Young Children's Learning *in* Theory And Practice Of Regressive Education (R Meighan), Educational Heretics Press 1993, ISBN 0 9518022 3 2

MEIGHAN, R; Never Too Late To Learn To Educate *in* Learning From Home Based Education (Ed. R. Meighan), Education Now 1992; ISBN 1 871526 06 X

MEIGHAN, J; Home Education Is Business As Usual *in* Learning From Home Based Education (Ed. R. Meighan), Education Now 1992; ISBN 1 871526 06 X

MERTTENS, R; Teaching Numeracy - Maths In The Primary Classroom, Scholastic Primary Professional Bookshelf 1997, ISBN 0 590 53429 7

MERTTENS, R; Primary Maths In Crisis - What Is To Be Done? *In* Teaching Numeracy - Maths In The Primary Classroom (Ed. R. Merttens), Scholastic Primary Professional Bookshelf 1997, ISBN 0 590 53429 7

MERTTENS, R; Reading Maths *In* Teaching Numeracy - Maths In The Primary Classroom (Ed. R. Merttens), Scholastic Primary Professional Bookshelf 1997, ISBN 0 590 53429 7

MERTTENS, R & BROWN, T; Number Operations And Procedures *In* Teaching Numeracy - Maths In The Primary Classroom (Ed. R. Merttens), Scholastic Primary Professional Bookshelf 1997, ISBN 0 590 53429 7

OTT, P; How To Detect And Manage Dyslexia, Heinemann Educational Publishers 1997, ISBN 0 435 104 195

PATTULLO, S; Deschooling Is Not Just For Children *in* Learning From Home Based Education (Ed. R. Meighan), Education Now 1992; ISBN 1 871526 06 X

PRINGLE. P; Adult Chauvinism And Children's Rights *in* Learning From Home Based Education (Ed. R. Meighan), Education Now 1992; ISBN 1 871526 06 X

RICH-SMITH, R; A Delightful Happening *in* Learning From Home Based Education (Ed. R. Meighan), Education Now 1992; ISBN 1 871526 06 X

ROUSHAM, L & ROWLAND, T; Numeracy And Calculators *In* Teaching Numeracy - Maths In The Primary Classroom (Ed. R. Merttens), Scholastic Primary Professional Bookshelf 1997, ISBN 0 590 53429 7

RUPIK, P; Putting Together A Home Based Education Package *in* Learning From Home Based Education (Ed. R. Meighan), Education Now 1992; ISBN 1 871526 06 X

SMITH, WO LESTER; Education, Penguin Books Ltd 1973

THOMAS, A; Educating Children At Home, Cassell Education 1998, ISBN 0 304 70180 7

TRAFFORD, B&K; Starting Out *in* Learning From Home Based Education (Ed. R. Meighan), Education Now 1992; ISBN 1 871526 06 X

WEBB, J; Studies Of Children Learning At Home *in* Learning From Home Based Education (Ed. R. Meighan), Education Now 1992; ISBN 1 871526 06 X

WEBB, J; Those Unschooled Minds: Home Educated Children Grow Up, Educational Heretics Press 1999; ISBN 1 900219 15 8

WHELDALL, D; WES *in* Learning From Home Based Education (Ed. R. Meighan), Education Now 1992; ISBN 1 871526 06 X

WILLIAMS, M & MOORE, W; Nuffield Maths 2 Teacher's Handbook, Longman Group Ltd. 1979 For Nuffield Foundation, ISBN 0582 188857

WILLIAMS, H; Developing Numeracy In The Early Years *In* Teaching Numeracy - Maths In The Primary Classroom (Ed. R. Merttens), Scholastic Primary Professional Bookshelf 1997, ISBN 0 590 53429 7

Index